What's in it for me?

MANCHESTER
1824

Manchester University Press

What's in it for me?

Self-interest and political difference

Thomas Prosser

Manchester University Press

The right of Thomas Prosser to be identified as the author of this work has been asserted by them in accordance with the Copyright, Designs and Patents Act 1988.

Published by Manchester University Press
Altrincham Street, Manchester M1 7JA
www.manchesteruniversitypress.co.uk

British Library Cataloguing-in-Publication Data
A catalogue record for this book is available from the British Library

ISBN 978 1 5261 5232 9 hardback
ISBN 978 1 5261 5231 2 paperback

First published 2021

The publisher has no responsibility for the persistence or accuracy of URLs for any external or third-party internet websites referred to in this book, and does not guarantee that any content on such websites is, or will remain, accurate or appropriate.

Typeset by Newgen Publishing UK

For Justyna and Marta

Contents

List of figures		viii
List of tables		ix
Acknowledgements		x
1	What's in it for me?	1
2	Are conservatives bastards?	32
3	Are Brexiters stupid?	54
4	Are liberal values wealthy values?	82
5	The new left: all about that base	107
6	Is social democracy finished?	131
Appendix: Devising a future research agenda		156
Bibliography		169
Index		193

Figures

5.1 Support for British parties by social grade,
1997–2019 (source: Ipsos Mori)   122

6.1 Vote share of social-democratic parties in
national elections (source: www.parlgov.org) 133

Tables

1.1 The worldviews   9

3.1 Brexit referendum voting by social grade   56

4.1 Voting in the French 2017 presidential
election first round by income   84

Acknowledgements

I give heartfelt thanks to Jon de Peyer, my editor at Manchester University Press. Jon has believed in this project since the start and his support has been instrumental. I must thank Manchester University Press generally. This is my second book with them and I have always been impressed by the professionalism and warmth of staff.

For comments which improved this book immensely, I am grateful to colleagues. In alphabetical order, I thank Leonardo Carella, Berwyn Davies, Peter Dorey, Leon Gooberman, Jonathan Kirkup, Guglielmo Meardi, Wojtek Paczos, Justyna Prosser, Lesley Prosser, Vera Šćepanović and Gareth Williams. Suggestions of four anonymous reviewers, procured by Manchester University Press, were invaluable. For help with charts and referencing, I thank Jac Larner and Omar Mohammed.

Chapter 1

What's in it for me?

It is rare for people to be asked the question which puts them squarely in front of themselves. (Arthur Miller, *The Crucible*)[1]

Why do people hold the political views that they do? Even if you have only a passing interest in politics, it is likely that you have thought about this question. If you are a Labour supporter, you might regard Conservatives as greedy. If you are a Brexiter, you may consider the views of Remainers to be driven by financial interest in EU membership. If you are a Remainer, you might think Brexiters are deluded. It is possible that you regard the foundations of your own views more charitably; many consider themselves guided by concern for the less fortunate or by the need to achieve national renewal.

Debates such as these will be familiar to anyone who is interested in politics. Though such discussions are diverse, they have one thing in common; they concern self-interest. There have always been disputes such as this in politics, yet in recent years they have intensified and we increasingly misunderstand the motives of others. It is this crisis which moved me to write this book. Why did Brexiters and Remainers vote as they did? What moves Conservative and Labour supporters as they head to polling booths? Who do different perspectives benefit?

My answer is almost as brief as the question. Most people gain something from their views. The reasons why this is the case are simple. We are evolved animals and, consistent with premises of a range of academic fields, tend to act in our self-interest.[2] Altruism may exist, scholars recognizing its evolutionary basis,[3] yet self-interest is an unescapable part of the human condition; it has characterized previous societies and will distinguish future ones. Contrary to common wisdom, *interests are at least as important as ideas* and structure politics in crucial ways. When this insight is applied to contemporary politics, one is confronted with puzzles. Why do richer citizens vote for parties which pledge to reduce inequality? Why would people who live in areas dependent on European funding detest the EU? Why do the well-to-do care passionately about Syrian asylum seekers?

The link between the interests of such citizens and these issues may often be indirect, yet associations become clearer if three influences are understood. Firstly, humans sometimes express interests in non-material terms. Scholars have long known that humans do not merely respond to economic incentives;

we also react to psychological stimuli.[4] Left-wing and liberal worldviews, which mobilize adherents against injustice, are associated with concerns such as care and fairness. Yet non-material values can be directly related to self-interest. In our globalized world, change disadvantages immobile populations; worldviews which activate values such as patriotism, as a means of controlling changes harmful to these citizens, are thus successful. Such goals are associated with national populism. Movements such as UKIP and the Brexit Party have emerged across developed countries in recent years and are popular because they arouse defensive emotions, associated with the non-material interests of supporters.

A second consideration is that human reasoning is limited. In recent years, scholars have recognized the imperfect evolution of the brain; our minds developed to meet challenges of primitive societies, not those of a complex global economy. We are also prone to overestimate our knowledge, an evolutionary phenomenon, associated with the need to have confidence in decisions, which means that we are unaware of the degree to which our preferences benefit ourselves.[5] This is sometimes the case with left-wing and liberal positions. Not only are these worldviews adopted on the basis of individual experience, meaning they subliminally reflect personal concerns, but limited resources result in altruistic elements of these perspectives losing ground to less magnanimous parts.

A third qualification is that worldviews have separate constituent parts, reflecting historical development.

Though most elements may be consistent with the interests of supporters, there may be aspects which lie in tension. Because of the way in which the latter parts have become embedded in the worldviews, normally over decades, they cannot be simply discarded. Individual beliefs therefore endure, accepted by supporters because they are parts of perspectives which broadly suit their interests.[6] Left-wing and national-populist movements provide examples. In the case of the left, there is long-standing focus on Israel, related to the anti-colonial history of the movement. It can be difficult to understand the attention which middle-class students lavish on the cause, yet this is a core belief of a movement which supports the economic aspirations of this group. The national-populist preoccupation with the EU has similar foundations. Though parts of Brexit threaten the interests of lower-class national populists, an economic downturn being one example, anti-Europeanism is a key element of a worldview which promises to preserve local conditions; this is in the interests of such citizens.

Why understanding self-interest is crucial

Serious discussion of self-interest is surprisingly rare. Though we ascribe this motive to opponents, we seldom reflect on our own self-interest, preferring to emphasize altruistic parts of our politics. Despite the importance of altruism, self-interest is so crucial a part of our nature that it cannot be ignored. Useful comparison may be made with sexuality, another integral part of the human character. Attempts to ignore or suppress sexuality are counterproductive; sad consequences of the repression of homosexuality or religiously imposed chastity show this. Most today recognize the need of humans to find outlets for natural urges, provided the rights of others are not violated. Awareness of self-interest is equivalent. Because of the impossibility of repressing self-interest, attempts to do so often cause frustration and chauvinism.

When one is aware of self-interest and exercises it in a way which respects the rights of others, healthy self-fulfilment encourages humility and moderation. Awareness of self-interest makes us more tolerant. People have always tended to misunderstand the motives of opponents, yet in recent years this has worsened; opponents are routinely depicted as selfish or treacherous. This is associated with the echo chambers of social media and moves away from political moderation.[7] Though there are several ways in which the motives of opponents can be better understood, appreciation of self-interest is one of the most promising. Awareness of one's own self-interest fosters reflectiveness. Self-interest is part of the human condition and present in all worldviews; when this is understood, positions tend to be advanced less aggressively. Appreciation of the self-interest of others is similar. If one realizes that opponents are not monsters, but humans with legitimate needs, it becomes easier to see humanity in adversaries.

Awareness of self-interest would also help move politics in a more liberal-democratic direction. For centuries, theories of liberal democracy have been based on the idea that interests of citizens are distinct yet legitimate. A liberal-democratic public sphere, in which different groups deliberate grievances to advance the common good,[8] attempts to resolve these differences. Authoritarians reject such methods. As Hannah Arendt and Karl Popper argued in the post-war years,[9] the authoritarian sees no humanity in opponents, regarding their desires as antithetical to the common good.

Despite the importance of deliberation, there has been pressure on the institutions which uphold this. In liberal democracies, parliaments and courts follow procedures which facilitate considered debate. Institutions such as presses and ombudsmen mediate citizen engagement in a related manner, structuring participation in a way which reinforces liberal-democratic standards. Such institutions are threatened by demands for more direct engagement in politics, reflecting factors such as distrust of politicians and the rise of social media. Even if there is need for reform of our institutions, radical articulation of these demands is concerning; liberal democracy has more successes than failures and alternatives have poor records.[10] Defence of liberal democracy is a wide project, involving multiple fronts, yet awareness of self-interest is crucial; it validates institutions which promote deliberation.

Recognition of different interests also allows for more effective cooperation. This paradox has long been recognized, international relations scholars emphasizing that global cooperation takes place when parties compromise to achieve a greater good.[11] If we recognized the goals of opponents as arising from legitimate self-interest, rather than as pathological, better cooperation would be possible. The issue of climate change, in which trade-offs must be made, is an example; concessions are more easily achieved if the aims of opponents are considered legitimate. It is no coincidence that the societies which have achieved the most advanced cooperation, namely the coordinated economies of Northern Europe, are characterized by less shrill public spheres. As the world faces crises such as COVID-19, such cooperation is imperative.

I base my argument on examination of five worldviews: (1) conservativism; (2) national populism; (3) liberalism; (4) the new left; and (5) social democracy. These are ideal types, corresponding loosely with party positions (see Table 1.1), yet embody main currents of thought in contemporary Britain. Most readers will identify with at least one. The worldviews vary in terms of support bases and positions on economic, social and international questions; this allows understanding of different expressions of self-interest and conditions in which contradictions occur. Grander terms such as 'philosophy' and 'ideology' are available, yet I prefer 'worldview'; this is a body of policy positions which reflects underlying values.[12] I sometimes use synonyms such as 'position' and 'perspective'.

Though I am an academic, this is not a purely academic book. It is one aimed at a wider readership which attempts to explain politics with reference to academic theories. Questions in individual chapters were selected for their relevance to contemporary politics and are broader than those normally addressed by academics. This results in tension between academic and popular definitions, most notably in the case of conservatism. I adopt definitions which balance emphases, explaining them in relevant chapters (see also Table 1.1). There is related tension in my understanding of support bases. I am primarily interested in voters motivated by these worldviews, though I consider activists when informative; selection is driven by specific questions. Benefits of writing for a wider audience are worth these choices; academics have yet to engage fully with renewed interest in politics. The fact that certain explanations will be counterintuitive to non-academics, reflecting differences in the interpretations of scholars and laypeople, makes this opportunity all the more attractive. I include an appendix which reflects on themes suitable for future research, consistent with my aim of investigating certain areas in greater detail. I hope this will influence other researchers.

Table 1.1 The worldviews

Worldview	Economic position (e.g. state intervention, redistribution)	Social position (e.g. immigration, LGBT+ rights)	International position (e.g. EU and NATO membership)	Support base	Associated parties/ movements	Definitional notes
Conservatism	Free market economy	Traditionalist	Although moderates advocate liberal multilateralism, some conservatives are nationalists	Small and large business owners; managers; older citizens; the very rich	Traditional wing of the Conservative Party	Conservatism is primarily concerned with opposition to change, yet a key influence on the Conservative Party is economic libertarianism. This position advocates limited state economic intervention and scholars do not consider it part of conservatism. Given the importance of economic libertarianism to the modern Conservative Party, I nonetheless include it in my definition of conservatism; this is in line with popular understandings[1]

(continued)

Table 1.1 (continued)

Worldview	Economic position (e.g. state intervention, redistribution)	Social position (e.g. immigration, LGBT+ rights)	International position (e.g. EU and NATO membership)	Support base	Associated parties/ movements	Definitional notes
National populism	Redistribution to lower classes; tax breaks for the very rich	Authoritarian	Opposed to multilateralism and Eurosceptic	Poor citizens in post-industrial and rural areas; the poorly educated; sections of the very rich	Johnsonian wing of the Conservative Party; the Brexit Party; UKIP; Vote Leave	I avoid pejorative terms and worried about use of the word 'populism'. Despite this concern, lack of alternative terms means that 'national populism' is most appropriate. 'Nativism' involves hostility to foreign influences[2] and 'nationalism'[3] is associated with external belligerence, yet neither capture the internal and external attitudes which interest me. 'National populism' is established in literature, Eatwell and Goodwin using it. Populism involves anti-elitism and preference for direct participation, studied movements adopting these stances[4]

Liberalism	Though the Liberal Democrats have a redistributive wing, most European liberal parties advocate non-intervention in the economy (i.e. economic libertarianism)	Liberal	Committed to liberal multilateralism	Socio-cultural professionals (e.g. doctors, teachers, social workers); the highly educated	The Liberal Democrats; People's Vote	I am interested in social liberalism. This emphasizes postmaterial values, involving freedom and autonomy, foreseeing a positive role for the state. An alternative meaning of liberalism, economic libertarianism, involves advocacy of free markets. I deal with this belief, associated with conservatism, in Chapter 2. Economic libertarian opposition to the state evokes objections of classic liberals, such liberals regarding state intervention as inimical to freedom[5]
New left	Public ownership and radical redistribution	Liberal, though immigration is increasingly debated	Anti-imperialist and particularly opposed to America, Israel and NATO. Older socialists are Eurosceptic, yet this is countered by enthusiasm of younger supporters	Students; young socio-cultural professionals; older socialists	Corbynite wing of the Labour Party; Momentum	The original new left was a movement which emerged in the 1950s, broadening traditional Marxism to include concerns such as civil rights and feminism.[6] Given time elapsed and difficulties associated with alternative terms, 'left-populist' being potentially pejorative, I use the term to refer to contemporary movements

(continued)

Table 1.1 (continued)

Worldview	Economic position (e.g. state intervention, redistribution)	Social position (e.g. immigration, LGBT+ rights)	International position (e.g. EU and NATO membership)	Support base	Associated parties/movements	Definitional notes
Social democracy	Mixed economy and moderate redistribution	Liberal, though immigration is increasingly debated	Committed to liberal multilateralism	Service and production workers; socio-cultural professionals	Traditional wing of the Labour Party; redistributive wing of the Liberal Democrats	I include New Labour in my understanding of social democracy. This is controversial, left-wingers emphasizing deregulatory measures of these governments, yet adaptation is core to social democracy; politicians such as Clement Attlee and Harold Wilson were criticized by contemporary left-wingers[7]

[1] These issues are discussed by N. O'Sullivan (2017) 'Conservatism', in M. Freeden, L. T. Sargent and M. Stears (eds), *The Oxford Handbook of Political Ideologies*. Oxford: Oxford University Press, 293–311; A. Gamble (2013) 'Economic Libertarianism', in M. Freeden, L. T. Sargent and M. Stears (eds), *The Oxford Handbook of Political Ideologies*. Oxford: Oxford University Press, 405–21.

[2] H. G. Betz (2017) 'Nativism Across Time and Space', *Swiss Political Science Review*, 23:4, 335–53.

[3] D. Woodwell (2007) *Nationalism in International Relations: Norms, Foreign Policy, and Enmity* New York: Springer.

[4] J.-W. Müller (2016) *What is Populism?* Philadelphia: University of Pennsylvania Press.

[5] R. Inglehart (1977) *The Silent Revolution: Changing Values and Political Styles among Western Publics*. Princeton: Princeton University Press, details postmaterial politics. Different forms of liberalism are identified by A. Vincent (1998) 'New Ideologies for Old?', *The Political Quarterly*, 69:1, 49–51.

[6] M. Kenny (1995) *The First New Left*. London: Lawrence & Wishart.

[7] B. Jackson (2013) 'Social Democracy', in M. Freeden, L. T. Sargent and M. Stears (eds), *The Oxford Handbook of Political Ideologies*. Oxford: Oxford University Press, 348–63.

The worldviews

Conservatism advocates free markets and tradition.[13] Support bases of conservative parties include capital owners and managers; a state which avoids economic intervention, leaving economic inequality intact, is in the interests of these citizens. This raises the question of whether conservative parties are solely agents of the rich. Though conscious self-interest explains the motivation of some conservative voters, such an interpretation is crude; many conservatives are motivated by moral concerns and consider conservatism to be in the general interest. Institutional influences, including the tendency of governments to pursue the common good, also impede such a goal. Conservatism thus demonstrates mediating influences upon self-interest with which we must be familiar.

Conservatism is riven by a fault line. Because free market policies associated with conservative self-interest often cause social discontent, those impoverished by conservative cuts seldom being tranquil, there are threats to order which conflict with conservative belief in tradition.[14] Conservatives propose several ways of resolving this difficulty, including charity and draconian law and order methods, which are at best ineffective and sometimes worsen such problems. This illustrates a problem affecting many worldviews, which I call externalization. Different citizens have varying interests, yet live in one world with finite resources; there is thus need for an equilibrium which satisfies separate interests. Externalization is a process in which the pursuit of self-interest by one group threatens prerogatives of others, jeopardizing the good of all.

National populism involves hostility to external influences, blaming immigrants, the EU and multinational firms for the problems of the common person. The worldview has become widespread in recent years and Nigel Farage and Donald Trump are adepts. National populism appeals to citizens with low income and education, yet its potential to damage these groups is well-known. The Brexit vote was a classic case; even though a British exit from the EU was considered likely to harm low-income voters, such groups tended to support Leave.[15] It is tempting to conclude that some engage in self-harm, yet this can be linked to the nonmaterial interests of such citizens. These groups have less capacity to adjust to a globalized world, related to their low skill profile, meaning that they favour worldviews which stress collective identity and preservation of local conditions.[16]

National populism suffers from serious externalities. Because the worldview stigmatizes others, reflecting energy generated in defence of local conditions, it causes internal and external disorder. The former involves victimization of minorities and is disagreeable, yet the latter is particularly serious; scapegoating of other states heightens international tension, increasing probability of conflict.[17]

Liberalism advocates individual rights to freedom and autonomy;[18] its British variant was most purely articulated by the Remain campaign and, despite referendum and election defeats, it remains a potent force. Owing to its emphasis on issues such as freedom of movement and equal opportunities, liberalism is often presented in ethical terms. Links with self-interest are nonetheless apparent. Because liberalism underlines rights such as freedom of movement and non-discrimination, it attracts socio-cultural professionals who benefit disproportionately. Liberalism thus defines ethics in terms consistent with the interests of richer classes; rather than stigmatizing wealth inequalities, an attitude which prevails in some tribal societies, liberals advocate equality of opportunities. Liberalism is currently undergoing crisis. Following long-standing association between liberalism and supranational organizations like the EU, the rise of national populism has made certain liberals less committed to national democracy.[19] This threatens the traditional balance between domestic and international liberal democracy, making reconciliation of diverse interests more difficult.

The new left advocates redistribution and equality;[20] in Britain, such views are associated with supporters of Jeremy Corbyn. The new left is descended from socialism, though important differences in support bases mean that the two are distinct. Working classes dominated socialist parties; young middle classes are relatively prominent in the new left. Though the new left advocates economic justice, there are good reasons for suspecting that its programme will primarily shift resources from the rich to the young middle classes, leaving the poorest in a similar position. This results from the new-left support base; no theory of redistribution, least of all the Marxist approaches which many in the new left favour, predicts that political movements will transfer resources away from supporters. This offers fascinating insight into the way in which self-interest furtively hijacks policy. Though talk is easy, the new left naturally emphasizing the justice of its programme, limited resources and subliminal tendency to prioritize personal need mean that resources tend to be transferred to supporters. The 2017 and 2019 Labour manifestos thus pledged to abolish tuition fees, a measure benefiting middle classes, while doing little to reverse Conservative benefit cuts.[21]

In a final chapter, I evaluate social democracy. This worldview seeks compromise between capitalism and socialism, advocating democratic collective action to achieve political and economic freedoms.[22] In Britain, the torch of social democracy has been carried by Labour moderates and certain Liberal Democrats. Social democrats have made undoubted mistakes, presiding over deregulation and unordered immigration. This is related to globalization, a process estranging social-democratic elites from concerns of traditional supporters. Social-democratic acceptance of capitalism, a long-standing left-wing criticism, is associated with such failures.[23]

Despite mistakes of social-democratic politicians and the challenge of globalization, social democracy has redeeming features. Emphasis on economic security means that it averts the instability associated with conservatism, while respect for individual rights counters national-populist stigmatization. Social democracy also avoids difficulties associated with the new left; restrained patriotism appeals to lower classes, while preference for gradual change avoids potential instability. In a way which other worldviews are not, social democracy is based on compromise, making it an appropriate governing tactic.[24]

Even if social democracy is in a period of crisis, its ability to correct the flaws of other positions means that its appeal may persist. History offers precedent of social-democratic renewal; after crisis in the 1930s, the worldview enjoyed a post-war golden age.[25] Perhaps this will not happen again. Because of divisions in the social-democratic base, between authoritarian lower classes and liberal middle classes, the worldview may have entered terminal decline. If this is the case, the ability of social democracy to reconcile separate interests might be emulated by alternative positions. It may be that another perspective considered in this work will don social-democratic clothes; stranger things have happened.

Explaining self-interest with institutional theory

Self-interest can be examined from several angles. Scientists recognize self-interest as a crucial aspect of natural selection, yet the existence of altruism in the natural world, e.g. in sterile worker ants, has led to debate over selective mechanisms. Early biologists emphasized group-based means, in which family members benefit from altruism, though later colleagues have proposed gene-based explanations, in which the costs of altruism are offset if recipients are genetic relations.[26] Self-interest has long interested social scientists. Though explanations involving altruism were traditionally considered unfeasible, recent decades have seen a change. Inspired by the work of the psychologist Daniel Batson, which shows that human motivation can be altruistic, altruism has been underlined by economists, psychologists and political scientists. Such approaches have encountered difficulty, the presumption of self-interest being engrained, yet the emphasis on altruism is welcome.[27]

I interpret human motives as mixed; self-interest is fundamental, even underpinning instances of 'altruism', yet genuine altruism is possible. Findings in several fields demonstrate this. Rather than engaging in general debates concerning self-interest and altruism, my interest in this book is the way in which contemporary worldviews reflect such tensions; I concentrate on the political expression of self-interest, in the context of early twenty-first-century globalization.

This necessitates engagement with scholarship on ideology,[28] a wide-ranging literature which underpins my analysis of tenets of the worldviews. Despite the importance of this work, my focus is distinct; I am interested in the question of how the worldviews satisfy needs of supporters. This entails analysis of such needs, their relationships with the worldviews and the ways in which such relationships evolve. There are several relevant approaches. Framing theory emphasizes ways in which elites shape public attitudes, stressing the unorganized nature of voter opinions. I draw lessons from this approach, yet institutional theory is most appropriate; this theory demonstrates the way in which politics satisfies different *needs*. Institutional theory is associated with political economy, a discipline which straddles political science and economics and in which I am expert. I research the relationship between support bases, institutions and ideas; more information on my background is in the appendix.[29]

Institutional theorists conceive institutions broadly; studied institutions range from language to table manners and include the worldviews evaluated in this book. Institutional theory shows why worldviews exist. A basic principle is that institutions fulfil specific functions, i.e. police provide order and schools educate citizens. For scholars, such language evokes functionalism; this theory was popular in post-war decades and proposed strong links between institutions and social need, interpreting society rather mechanically. Functionalism has now waned, related to its deterministic nature and tendency to underplay conflict. I am not a functionalist, yet the decline of this approach does not mean that we should reject all reference to functions; scholars continue to emphasize that institutions fulfil needs.[30]

Recognition of associations between institutions and functions allows the establishment of provisional relationships between worldviews and self-interest. As I note above, humans are self-interested; I therefore assume that there is a link between worldviews and the interests of supporters. This is admittedly crude and I make caveats below. The opposite assumption, that there is no necessary association between worldviews and interests, is more problematic. Given that worldviews considered in this book have long-term relationships with certain groups, spanning centuries and continents, it is difficult to believe that there is no link.

A theory called historical institutionalism addresses problems with functionalism, allowing understanding of conditional relationships between self-interest and worldviews. Historical institutionalists agree that founding processes known as 'critical junctures' exert disproportionate influence on institutions, locking them into developmental paths. A classic example is the qwerty keyboard. The American inventor Christopher Latham Sholes adopted this inefficient design in the 1870s, with the aim of slowing typing speeds; contemporary typewriters jammed if inputs were too rapid. Despite this anomaly, transition costs have prohibited subsequent change; the institution of typing has thus been shaped by a quirk of its critical juncture.[31]

Critical junctures of the worldviews took place around the nineteenth century, the worldviews developing as traditional societies industrialized.

Though ultimately reflecting needs of social classes, founders of worldviews such as Adam Smith, Karl Marx and John Stuart Mill were influential at the time of critical junctures. The worldviews achieved consequent impact on human history, shaping societies across the globe. Historical institutionalists analyse subsequent processes of development, emphasizing the importance of 'path dependency'. This implies that past decisions make specific paths appropriate, even if historic conditions no longer apply. Qwerty is an example of this; early automobile designs and competing standards for electric currents are others.[32] Yet conditions of birth result in imperfect fit with certain contexts; conservatives who desire financial security struggle with free market aspects of conservatism, while there is tension between Marxism and the affluence of new-left support bases.

Consistent with institutional theory, I pay attention to socio-economic factors such as income and occupation. Across the social sciences, researchers privilege explanations which are rooted in analysis of structural influences such as these. This raises question about the influence of ideas. Though political ideas are highly significant, mobilizing populations and propelling events in unforeseen directions, the tradition in which I write considers them subservient to material interests.[33] Debates about the abolition of slavery are instructive. Though few would deny the role played by Christian compassion in ending the trade, the rise of capitalism, and the consequent need for a more productive labour force, is considered most significant; for many centuries, slavery existed in Christian societies. A precondition to the emergence and success of abolitionist ideas was structural changes to the economy, even if the ideas themselves had a mobilizing influence.[34] Max Weber compared ideas to 'switchmen, determin[ing] the tracks along which action has been pushed by the dynamic of interest'.[35]

In recent years, there has been greater emphasis upon the influence of ideas. Discursive institutionalism, a new form of institutional theory associated with the political scientist Vivien Schmidt, emphasizes the importance of ideas and their capacity to inspire change. This argument has inspired studies of diverse areas, from gay rights to the governance of the Eurozone.[36] Despite such developments, most institutional theorists continue to regard structural influences as most relevant. I share this interpretation, though recognize the importance of ideas.

Different structural influences upon individuals and classes need be clarified. In individual cases, views can be held which lie in tension with socio-economic status. There were doubtless miners who supported Thatcher; such curiosities can be attributed to factors such as religiosity, aspiration or simple contrarianism. Among my readers, there may be educated, ethnic minority Brexiters or poor, older Remainers. There is more space for manoeuvre in individual cases, allowing for convictions which have a looser relationship with structural forces.

Yet this is unfeasible for entire classes. There are a vast number of people involved, which implies that idiosyncrasies subside. The process is similar to biological evolution. In this field, scientists emphasize that evolved characteristics are a response to the physical environment, for example animal coloration. There are too many organisms involved in evolutionary processes for advantageous traits to appear independently of the environment. Similarly, researchers conclude that political views which are common to classes of persons are based in socio-economic conditions. Not only are too many people involved for it to be otherwise, but the appearance of these trends across countries makes this more unfeasible.[37]

Despite these caveats, certain preferences lie in tension with my explanations. To give one example, 40 per cent of lower-class voters supported Remain, while 43 per cent of higher-class voters favoured Leave (see Table 3.1); this goes beyond anomalies. Many cases can be explained. Poor ethnic minorities might recoil at anti-immigrant sentiments, while rich businessowners may be averse to European regulation. I explain exceptions when possible, associated paradoxes nuancing my argument. Yet the diversity of such categories is considerable. Some await detailed investigation, while others appear inexplicable. I therefore focus on general explanations, which provide a framework for understanding exceptions; scholars are familiar with trade-offs between generalization and precision.[38] Studies of specific cases, some of which are suggested in the appendix, will achieve greater exactness.

Similarities across countries show the significance of particular trends. I am most aware of this; in my academic career, I research the development of political economies across Europe. In this book, I nonetheless concentrate on Britain. Not only am I a citizen and resident of the country, meaning that I am particularly familiar with developments, but the British case offers fascinating examples of relevant trends. Related phenomena in other countries should not be forgotten. Aside from being interesting in themselves, different contexts show whether developments in Britain are general or particular.

In writing such a book, I can scarcely complain if readers examine my own profile for underpinning motivations. Some will associate the fact that I say little about race and gender with my status as a white, heterosexual male. Though I do not agree that this invalidates my right to discuss certain issues, as some assert,[39] I accept the importance of such characteristics; in recent decades, a series of writers have shown how these traits underpin power structures.[40] I hope that others reflect on the relevance of my arguments for these categories; many of the concepts I develop, such as the tendency for movements to relegate certain causes to secondary priorities, are relevant to these debates. On the other hand, race and gender are traits which inform approaches to politics, rather than the developed worldviews which are considered in this book.

Readers will disagree with some of my arguments; this is inevitable and I welcome it. I hope that disagreements are constructive. Throughout this book, I attempt to adopt a conciliatory tone. Not only do I avoid pejorative terms, but I empathize with adherents of different worldviews. Supporters of these positions may think that I am sometimes unfair, yet I hope they accept that this reflects genuine disagreement rather than malice.

Perhaps I will convert few who initially disagree with me. It may be unwise to expect otherwise. Studies show that we are attached to our views,[41] reflecting social and emotional resources sunk in these positions. My aim is more modest; I would merely like to make readers reflect. Introspection might involve acknowledgement that our preferred positions are not completely altruistic and/or that our opponents are not entirely malign. In an increasingly partisan culture, we are losing this capacity; this is a worrying development for those who value civic deliberation. Self-interest is a perfect topic for reflection. Despite the ubiquity of self-interest, we tend not to discuss it in a sophisticated way. It is high time that this changed.

Notes

1 Arthur Miller (2003) *The Crucible*. London: Penguin, 21.
2 Such debates are outlined by Stephanie L. Brown, R. Michael Brown and Louis A. Penner (eds) (2011) *Moving beyond Self-Interest: Perspectives from Evolutionary Biology, Neuroscience, and the Social Sciences*. Oxford: Oxford University Press.

3 Richard Dawkins (1976) *The Selfish Gene*. Oxford: Oxford University Press; Frans B. M. De Waal (2008) 'Putting the Altruism Back Into Altruism: The Evolution of Empathy', *Annual Review of Psychology*, 59:1, 279–99.

4 These controversies are introduced from a psychological perspective by Jonathan Haidt (2012) *The Righteous Mind: Why Good People are Divided by Politics and Religion*. New York: Random House. There is also much work on non-material voting motivations, e.g. Joseph R. Gusfield (1986) *Symbolic Crusade: Status Politics and the American Temperance Movement*. Chicago: University of Illinois Press; Ronald Inglehart (1977) *The Silent Revolution: Changing Values and Political Styles among Western Publics*. Princeton: Princeton University Press; Seymour Martin Lipset (1981) *Political Man: The Social Bases of Politics*. Baltimore: Johns Hopkins University Press.

5 Cognitive science is introduced by Hannah Critchlow (2019) *The Science of Fate: Why Your Future is More Predictable Than You Think*. London: Hachette Publishing. The evolution of overconfidence is discussed by Dominic D. P. Johnson and James H. Fowler (2011) 'The Evolution of Overconfidence', *Nature*, 477:1, 317–20.

6 This is consistent with historical institutionalism, elaborated by Kathleen Thelen (1999) 'Historical Institutionalism in Comparative Politics', *Annual Review of Political Science*, 2:1, 369–404. I explain the approach later in the chapter.

7 Gina Masullo-Chen and Shuning Lu (2017) 'Online Political Discourse: Exploring Differences in Effects of Civil and Uncivil Disagreement in News Website Comments', *Journal of Broadcasting & Electronic Media*, 61:1, 108–25; Yascha Mounk (2018) *The People vs. Democracy: Why Our Freedom is in Danger and How to Save it*. Cambridge, MA: Harvard University Press.

8 A classic definition of the common good refers to 'a good proper to, and attainable only by, the community, yet individually shared by its members', Louis Dupré (1993) 'The Common Good and the Open Society', *The Review of Politics*, 55:4, 687–712. Though critics assert that the

common good is subject to sectional interpretations, the term remains important. My definition is minimalistic and includes basic security, economic growth and environmental protection.

9 Classic texts include Hannah Arendt (1951) *The Origins of Totalitarianism*. New York: Harcourt Brace Jovanovich; Karl Raimund Popper (1945) *The Open Society and its Enemies*. London: Routledge.

10 A series of recent books discuss such issues at length, e.g. Mounk, *The People vs. Democracy*; David Runciman (2018) *How Democracy Ends*. London: Profile Books.

11 Robert Jervis (1999) 'Realism, Neoliberalism, and Cooperation: Understanding the Debate', *International Security*, 24:1, 42–63.

12 The meaning of political values is elaborated by Paul Goren (2005) 'Party Identification and Core Political Values', *American Journal of Political Science*, 49:4, 881–96.

13 Classic tenets of conservatism are introduced by Noel O'Sullivan (2013) 'Conservatism', in M. Freeden, L. T. Sargent and M. Stears (eds), *The Oxford Handbook of Political Ideologies*. Oxford: Oxford University Press, 293–311, while economic libertarian aspects of the worldview are summarized by Andrew Gamble (2013) 'Economic Libertarianism', in M. Freeden, L. T. Sargent and M. Stears (eds), *The Oxford Handbook of Political Ideologies*. Oxford: Oxford University Press, 405–21. Table 1.1 outlines definitional challenges. Support bases of conservative parties are discussed by Daniel Oesch (2008) 'The Changing Shape of Class Voting: An Individual-Level Analysis of Party Support in Britain, Germany and Switzerland', *European Societies*, 10:3, 329–55.

14 A classic source is Karl Polanyi (1994) *The Great Transformation*. New York: Farrar & Rinehart.

15 A key source on the profile of Brexit voters is Sara B. Hobolt (2016) 'The Brexit Vote: A Divided Nation, a Divided Continent', *Journal of European Public Policy*, 23:9, 1259–77. Other important studies include Tak Wing Chan, Morag Henderson, Maria Sironi and Juta Kawalerowicz (2017) 'Understanding the Social and Cultural Bases of Brexit',

Department of Quantitative Social Science, University College London; Matthew Goodwin and Oliver Heath (2016) 'The 2016 Referendum, Brexit and the Left Behind: An Aggregate-Level Analysis of the Result', *The Political Quarterly*, 87:3, 323–32; Neil Lee, Katy Morris and Thomas Kemeny (2018) 'Immobility and the Brexit Vote', *Cambridge Journal of Regions, Economy and Society*, 11:1, 143–63.

16 David Goodhart (2017) *The Road to Somewhere: The Populist Revolt and the Future of Politics*. London: C. Hurst & Co.

17 This is consistent with liberal internationalist interpretations, e.g. Anne-Marie Slaughter (2004) *A New World Order*. Princeton: Princeton University Press.

18 Support bases of liberal parties are discussed by Michael Freeden and Marc Stears (2013) 'Liberalism', in M. Freeden, L. T. Sargent and M. Stears (eds), *The Oxford Handbook of Political Ideologies*. Oxford: Oxford University Press, 329–47; Herbert Kitschelt (1994) *The Transformation of European Social Democracy*. Cambridge: Cambridge University Press; Oesch, 'Changing Shape'.

19 Undemocratic liberalism is discussed by Mounk, *The People vs. Democracy*. For liberal critiques of democracy, see Jason Brennan (2016) *Against Democracy*. Princeton: Princeton University Press; David Harsanyi (2014) *The People Have Spoken (and They Are Wrong): The Case Against Democracy*. Washington, DC: Regnery; David Van Reybrouck (2016) *Against Elections: The Case for Democracy*. London: Bodley Head.

20 Chantal Mouffe (2018) *For a Left Populism*. London: Verso Books.

21 Torsten Bell (2017) 'For Labour, It's All About What You Say', Resolution Foundation. Available at: www.resolutionfoundation.org/comment/for-labour-its-all-about-what-you-say/. Accessed 16 May 2020; Jane Gingrich and Silja Häusermann (2015) 'The Decline of the Working-Class Vote, the Reconfiguration of the Welfare Support Coalition and Consequences for the Welfare State', *Journal of European Social Policy*, 25:3, 50–75.

22 Ben Jackson (2013) 'Social Democracy', in M. Freeden, L. T. Sargent and M. Stears (eds), *The Oxford Handbook of Political Ideologies*. Oxford: Oxford University Press, 348–63.

23 David Bailey, Jean-Michel de Waele, Fabien Escalona and Mathieu Vieira (eds) (2016) *European Social Democracy During the Global Economic Crisis*. Manchester: Manchester University Press; Ashley Lavelle (2016) *The Death of Social Democracy: Political Consequences in the 21st Century*. London: Routledge.

24 Thomas Meyer and Lewis Hinchman (2007) *The Theory of Social Democracy*. Cambridge: Polity.

25 Tony Judt (2006) *Postwar: A History of Europe since 1945*. New York: Penguin.

26 Dawkins, *The Selfish Gene*; J. Philippe Rushton, Robin J. H. Russell and Pamela Wells (1984) 'Genetic Similarity Theory: Beyond Kin Selection', *Behaviour Genetics*, 14:3, 179–93.

27 Multiple sources discuss self-interest in general terms. Brown et al., *Moving beyond Self-Interest*, is an edited collection which provides interdisciplinary perspective. Self-interest is also discussed in academic journals; there are recent contributions in fields such as political science, economics and psychology, e.g. Douglas A. Bosse and Robert A. Phillips (2016) 'Agency Theory and Bounded Self-Interest', *Academy of Management Review*, 41:2, 276–97; Valerie Braithwaite (2009) 'Attitudes to Tax Policy: Politics, Self-interest and Social Values', Research Note 9, Centre for Tax System Integrity. Australian National University, Canberra; Mark R. Hoffarth and John T. Jost (2017) 'When Ideology Contradicts Self-Interest: Conservative Opposition to Same-Sex Marriage among Sexual Minorities – a Commentary on Pinsof and Haselton', *Psychological Science*, 28:10, 1521–24; Sungmin Rho and Michael Tomz (2017) 'Why Don't Trade Preferences Reflect Economic Self-Interest?', *International Organization*, 71:1, 85–108. Notable work of Batson includes a book, Daniel Batson (2011) *Altruism in Humans*. New York: Oxford University Press.

28 A valuable source is Freeden and Stears, 'Liberalism'.

29 Framing theory is discussed by Dennis Chong and James N. Druckman (2007) 'Framing Theory', *Annual Review of Political Science*, 10:1, 103–26. Institutional theory is introduced by Guy B. Peters (2019) *Institutional Theory in Political Science: The New Institutionalism*. Cheltenham: Edward Elgar.

30 Functionalism is introduced by Paul Colomy (1990) *Functionalist Sociology*. Cheltenham: Edward Elgar. Continuity between functionalism and institutional theory is emphasized by Stewart Clegg (2010) 'The State, Power, and Agency: Missing in Action in Institutional Theory?', *Journal of Management Inquiry*, 19:1, 4–13; Wolfgang Streeck (2005) 'Rejoinder: On Terminology, Functionalism (Historical) Institutionalism and Liberalization', *Socio-Economic Review*, 3:3, 577–87.

31 Thelen, 'Historical Institutionalism' introduces historical institutionalism. A definitive account of critical junctures is provided by Giovanni Capoccia and Daniel Kelemen (2007) 'The Study of Critical Junctures: Theory, Narrative, and Counterfactuals in Historical Institutionalism', *World Politics*, 59:3, 341–69.

32 Paul Pierson (2000) 'Increasing Returns, Path Dependence, and the Study of Politics', *American Political Science Review*, 94:2, 251–67.

33 A tendency regretted by Vivien A. Schmidt (2008) 'Discursive Institutionalism: The Explanatory Power of Ideas and Discourse', *Annual Review of Political Science*, 11:1, 303–26.

34 David Brion Davis (1999) *The Problem of Slavery in The Age of Revolution, 1770–1823*. Oxford: Oxford University Press.

35 Max Weber, Hans Heinrich Gerth and C. Wright Mills (1946) *Max Weber: Essays in Sociology*. Oxford: Oxford University Press, 280. Though some contend that this quote has been misinterpreted, this is not of special concern; the point is that subsequent scholars have advocated this interpretation. See Jonathan Eastwood (2005) 'The Role of Ideas in Weber's Theory of Interests', *Critical Review*, 17:2, 89–100.

36 Kelly Kollman (2014) 'Deploying Europe: The Creation of Discursive Imperatives for Same-Sex Unions', in D. Paternotte and P. Ayoub (eds), *LGBT Activism and the Making of Europe*. London: Palgrave Macmillan, 97–118; Vivien A. Schmidt (2014) 'Speaking to the Markets or to the People? A Discursive Institutionalist Analysis of the EU's Sovereign Debt Crisis', *The British Journal of Politics and International Relations*, 16:1, 188–209.

37 Animal coloration is discussed by Martin Stevens, Innes C. Cuthill, Amy M. M. Windsor and Hannah J. Walker (2006) 'Disruptive Contrast in Animal Camouflage', *Proceedings of the Royal Society B: Biological Sciences*, 273:1600, 2433–8. Important analysis of similarities between biological and institutional evolution is undertaken by Orion Lewis and Sven Steinmo (2012) 'How Institutions Evolve: Evolutionary Theory and Institutional Change', *Polity*, 44:3, 314–39. Significantly, they do not use biological evolution as a metaphor but assert that it is one example of 'generalized Darwinism', a perspective which argues that evolution is not confined to biology (315).

38 Geoff Payne and Malcolm Williams (2005) 'Generalization in Qualitative Research', *Sociology*, 39:2, 295–314.

39 Reni Eddo-Lodge (2018) *Why I'm No Longer Talking to White People about Race*. London: Bloomsbury.

40 This argument is a staple of poststructuralism. Among such scholars, the work of Michel Foucault is notable, e.g. Michel Foucault (1990) *The History of Sexuality: An Introduction, Volume I*. New York: Vintage; Michel Foucault (2012) *Discipline and Punish: The Birth of the Prison*. New York: Vintage.

41 Haidt, *The Righteous Mind* discusses this in general terms. There are also specific studies, e.g. Brendan Nyhan and Jason Reifler (2010) 'When Corrections Fail: The Persistence of Political Misperceptions', *Political Behaviour*, 32:2, 303–30.

Chapter 2

Are conservatives bastards?

Is there some society you know that doesn't run on greed? You think Russia doesn't run on greed? You think China doesn't run on greed? What is greed? Of course, none of us are greedy, it's only the other fellow who's greedy. The world runs on individuals pursuing their separate interests. (Milton Friedman)[1]
Venal
Old
Tory
Etonians
Conniving
Odious
Neo nazi
Self serving
Egotistical
Reckless
Vermin
And
Twatty
Idiotic
Vile
Evil
Scum. (Kazzia, @KazzJenkins)

Conservatives are bastards. This kind of verdict, often phrased in fruitier language, has long been accepted wisdom among sections of the left; the rise of social media and Jeremy Corbyn merely pronounced this trend. Such assertions reflect the conviction that conservatives are selfish. Critics point to the long-standing association between the Conservative Party and the rich, leading to policies which are favourable to wealthier citizens. Aside from claims that Conservatives are more likely to introduce tax cuts and deregulation, many go further; on social media, there are allegations that Conservatives wish to privatize the NHS or purge the poor with COVID-19.

Much of this is very crude. Conspiracy theories aside, the NHS has survived decades of Conservative rule. Certain assertions nonetheless contain grains of truth. For many years, the Conservative Party has relied on richer voters, who in turn expect the party to introduce policies consistent with their interests. The relationship between the Conservative Party and richer classes has been evident throughout modern times, though it became particularly apparent during the Thatcher governments. In these years, Conservatives aggressively lowered taxes and deregulated markets to satisfy their wealthy support base. There are similar parties in other developed countries. Some are more moderate, such as the German Christian Democratic Union, whereas others are more radical, such as the US Republican Party.[2]

It is true that conservative values concern more than economics. In Britain, a variety of groups who are resistant to change belong to the Conservative Party; these include rural and religious communities. Such cases show the importance of non-material influences. Because of strong attachment to localities and/or particular values, the politics of certain citizens are less sensitive to economic incentives. There is evidence that such groups are expanding, low-income voters increasingly attracted to Johnsonian conservatism.[3]

Separate non-economic and economic agendas present definitional problems. Though political scientists consider the former to be authentically conservative, they label the latter economic libertarian or neoliberal. Given that the Conservative Party is synonymous with such economic policies, I include economic libertarianism in my definition of (small-c) conservatism. This demonstrates tensions between economic and non-economic aspects of conservatism, which I explore in this chapter.[4]

Why conservatism is broader than self-interest

If this wider definition is accepted, modern conservatism exhibits a clear relationship with economic self-interest. The precise nature of this relationship is nonetheless contingent. There are intellectual and institutional filters, the conservative worldview being wider than mere self-interest and the institutions of government implying care for the common good, which ensure that conservative self-interest is indirectly realized. These constraints are relevant to all worldviews, meaning that conservatism demonstrates mediating influences with which we must be familiar. Despite these nuances, there is one fact which must be stated baldly; many conservative voters are motivated by conscious self-interest. Conservatism is popular among groups such as small and large business owners and managers. Clear command structures in such occupations are related to conservative cultural views, yet economic motives are central. The low tax and regulatory burdens associated with conservatism benefit such citizens.[5]

The relationship between conservatism and the self-interest of the rich provokes debate. Left-wingers hold scathing views of the Conservative Party; on social media, Labour supporters denounce conservatives for their selfishness. Though the deregulatory policies supported by conservatives are problematic – I argue below that they cause instability – defence of the interests of supporters is not unique to conservatives; it is a practice in which all parties engage. The traditional ability of left-wing parties to curb inequality was related to poorer electoral bases, rather than the moral qualities of leaders and supporters. The conscious self-interest of some conservatives is nonetheless unattractive; the way in which this behaviour entrenches existing inequalities, as opposed to the self-interest of poorer citizens, makes it antisocial. At policy level, those Conservative measures which flout orthodoxy also grate. The pension triple lock, a coalition policy which for electoral reasons protected pensioners from austerity, is one example; if conservative belief in the small state is to be fair, it must be applied consistently.

Whatever the behaviour of certain conservatives, two caveats about the nature of conservatism must be made. Firstly, there is more to the conservative worldview than self-interest. Ideas have a life of their own, following peculiar developmental paths and embodying more than rational calculation.[6] This is illustrated by the evolution of conservative thought. From the end of the eighteenth century, thinkers such as Adam Smith argued for the primacy of private property. Friedrich Hayek and Milton Friedman continued this tradition in modern times, defending capital from socialist attacks.[7] It is crucial to note that these authorities did not write with material goals in mind. Such writers had intellectual and ethical aims and developed a rich body of conservative thought; this tradition conceives of self-reliance in moral terms and advocates a state which facilitates this end.

These ideas became popular because they were convenient to wealthier citizens. As I explain in Chapter 4, there is an important link between ideas and interests. Though some conservative voters do not genuinely believe in such ideas, supporting conservative parties for financial reasons and favouring measures like the triple lock when economic libertarianism threatens their interests, other conservatives are different. The behaviour of conservative activists, a group distinct from voters, is revealing.[8] Rather than engaging in politics for economic reasons, activists genuinely believe in conservative ideas of self-reliance; the moral principles of Thatcherism are a continued inspiration. The equation of conservatism with selfishness is thus reductive. There are numerous conservatives who are motivated by moral concerns and consider conservatism to be in the general interest. This influence of ideas is relevant to all perspectives, implying that worldviews must be understood in their own terms; in later chapters, we shall see the vigour of other ideas.

A second caveat is that conservatism shows that governing parties do not *merely* serve the interests of supporters; institutional influences must be considered. When in office, governing parties are obliged to advance the common good; this is a result of the wider duties of government.[9] Quite aside from areas such as defence, in which geopolitical realities and alliances constrain governments, economic policy is framed with reference to the common good; this is ensured by institutions such as the Bank of England, which guard against excessive politicization. The Civil Service is also crucial, many underestimating its role during the COVID-19 crisis. Though some argue that Conservative governments are different, riding roughshod over opponents to enrich supporters,[10] there is limited evidence for this. Not only have policies in the one nation tradition improved conditions for the poorest, but certain decisions have angered the party base. The Cameron government's means-testing of child benefit, which disadvantaged richer recipients, is a case in point. The left is not exempt from similar challenges. In several cases, Attlee, Mitterrand and Syriza governments being famous examples, it has been discovered that governments must forsake bases to advance the common good.

The most caustic assessments of conservatism are thus problematic. Even if certain conservative voters are self-interested, consequently worsening inequalities, many conservatives sincerely believe in self-reliance. It is a shame that scathing attitudes are common on the left; such attitudes, prevalent on social media, sow discord and frustrate cooperation. It is no coincidence that in societies in which cooperation is most advanced, namely the coordinated economies of Northern Europe, attitudes towards conservatives are less hostile. On the other hand, conservatives are more moderate in these contexts.

Conservatism and inequality: a contradictory relationship?

Despite the contingent relationship between conservatism and self-interest, effects of conservatism present a different problem. In this sense, conservatism demonstrates a crucial principle which is relevant to other worldviews; this is a phenomenon which I call externalization.[11] Humans have distinct interests, yet live in one world with finite resources. As is well known, humankind disputes these resources; innumerable wars, not to mention quarrels which fall short of armed conflict, have resulted from this problem. If we are to live peaceably, a way must be found to reconcile competing interests; this is particularly true in a globalized world. In my opinion, certain worldviews do not do this successfully. Externalization involves a process in which the pursuit of self-interest by one group threatens the welfare of others, jeopardizing the good of all.

The most dramatic instances of externalization are associated with national populism. As I argue in Chapter 3, the potential of national populism to create tension between countries means that it is particularly destabilizing. Conservatism is nonetheless prone to its own form of externalization, which is relevant to contemporary politics and is an Achilles' heel of the worldview. This is the tendency of conservatism to create inequality.

Across the West in recent decades, the deregulatory measures which are favoured by conservatives have tended to increase inequality. In Britain, inequality grew markedly in the early 1980s, associated with Thatcher reforms. Though overall levels have since remained steady,[12] certain groups have been badly affected; these include the long-term unemployed and young middle classes. Many groups have become trapped in dangerously precarious conditions, COVID-19 making this evident. In recent times, the income of the top 1 per cent has expanded,[13] CEO-average worker salary ratios rising from 45:1 in the mid-1990s to 129:1 in 2016.[14] A series of drivers have encouraged such trends. Not only have reductions in benefits fuelled inequality, but rising property prices have excluded certain groups from the housing market. Though many of these tendencies are related to structural influences associated with globalization, Conservative governments have been far from innocent, advocating the shrinking of the state. In comparison to Western sister parties, the Conservative Party has embraced deregulation particularly keenly. This is associated with self-interest, the Conservative base facilitating policies which benefit wealthier supporters.[15]

Inequality is associated with negative trends. As evidenced by research, unequal societies are more prone to problems such as obesity and addiction.[16] The basis of this relationship is clear; as life becomes more insecure, the desire for short-term gratification increases. Related to this, unequal societies are more dangerous; the reader might reflect on whether they would prefer to stroll late at night in Mexico City or Copenhagen.[17] Damaging as such developments are, there is one consequence of inequality which undermines the internal consistency of conservatism and means that, even by its own logic, conservatism has difficulty reconciling self-interest with the common good. This is the tendency of inequality to threaten order. I concentrate on this effect not only because it is vital to conservatism, demonstrating tension between economic and non-economic aspects of the worldview, but also due to consequences for global stability.

To an extent to which other worldviews do not, conservatism places a premium on order. From at least the time of Edmund Burke, a late eighteenth-century philosopher who recoiled at revolutionary violence in France, emphasis has been placed upon the preservation of institutions.[18] Conservatives argue that ruptures with established institutions risk discarding their best aspects, endangering political stability. There is much in this, particularly when the institutions are liberal-democratic ones; it is difficult to think of an instance in which the overthrow of liberal-democratic institutions has led to a better alternative. Social democrats and liberals thus use aspects of this argument, particularly in countries such as Germany which are historically prone to instability. It is especially relevant in a globalized world. Given increased interconnectedness, disorder in one country has greater potential to disrupt elsewhere.

The relationship between free market economics and disorder has long been acknowledged. In the *Great Transformation*, interwar economist Karl Polanyi noted the instability of nineteenth-century British capitalism,[19] arguing that social conditions associated with unregulated markets encouraged challenges to the system such as rural riots and Chartism. Polanyi lived through similar processes; the rise of extremists of the 1930s reflected reluctance to intervene in failing markets. These experiences marked post-war conservatives, such as Conservative Prime Minister Harold Macmillan, who rejected economic libertarianism. The problem endures to this day. Even if the liberalization of markets has produced economic growth, accompanying inequality has caused serious unrest.

In the West, the most visible symptom has been the rise of anti-establishment parties; in recent years, left- and right-wing radicals have won increasing support. The emergence of these parties is related to the stagnation of living standards. Globalization has had its successes, millions having been lifted out of poverty in developing countries,[20] yet the relative position of the middle and working classes in developed countries has declined. Since the economic crisis, wage growth has been weak; in the UK, the real wages of the median worker fell by almost 5 per cent from 2008 to 2017.[21] Despite these developments, the rich have fared comparatively well. Trends are complex, income inequality remaining steady in Britain,[22] yet the income share of the rich has increased in most contexts; international data show a comparative rise in the household incomes of the richest 10 per cent.[23]

Relative declines are particularly significant. Humans can be happy with fewer resources than we enjoy today; contentedness of post-war decades, a period marked by austere yet rising standards, is evidence of this. In our time, the tendency for middle-income citizens to lose ground to the rich is particularly relevant. Humans hate loss of status; this reflects primordial anxieties and can be observed in every society. Relative deprivation theory recognizes this. Developed in the mid-twentieth century by Garry Runciman, the theory states that human proximity to resources which they believe to be in their reach, yet cannot obtain, is a key cause of discontent.[24]

Conservative economic policies are closely linked to recent relative declines. Housing and labour market policy has tended to disadvantage groups such as the upper working and lower middle classes; young members have particularly suffered. Independent of questions of justice, the political implications of these processes are key. Middle-income groups are politically crucial, comprising electoral bases of established parties. Discontent among these voters has thus proved a boon for anti-establishment parties; in recent years, these movements have grown across the West. There is no iron link between the success of these parties and decline of living standards, national-populist movements prospering in several buoyant contexts, yet research suggests that Western politics is increasingly affected by this loop; recent studies find that national populism reflects comparative hardship within generally favourable economic contexts and perception of loss of status.[25]

Anti-establishment parties undermine internal and external order. In terms of the former, the radical tendency to create enemies causes internal unrest; this is compounded by disdain for parliamentary procedure, related to the preference of these movements for popular legitimacy.[26] In terms of the latter, such parties cause external tension through conflict with neighbouring countries. This is particularly true of national populists and, in Chapter 3, I examine this issue. Brexit encapsulates many of these threats. The policy breaks long-established relations with a premier international organization, because of a referendum which bypassed parliament. Implementation has threatened public order; the prospect of no deal, raising the spectre of shortages of basic supplies and riots, was one example. It is thus difficult to reconcile Brexit with conservatism. Though many who support Brexit identify as conservatives, the associated disorder and institutional rupture make this difficult to credit; this interpretation is validated by the initial opposition of most Conservative MPs. Popularity of Brexit among grassroots Conservatives and sections of the parliamentary party rather indicates a drift towards national populism, consuming the entire Conservative Party under Boris Johnson.[27]

National-populist self-interest is associated with continuity of local conditions. Because of their limited mobility, citizens with low income and education prefer a world in which change is slower. Conservative voters increasingly correspond to this profile, the party winning historic support among low-income citizens in the 2019 election (see Figure 5.1). Given that such voters also prefer redistributive measures, contrary to conservative orthodoxy, there is potential for discord in the Conservative support base. I evaluate this in Chapter 5, arguing that although the existence of poorer supporters will make the Johnson government more redistributive, changes will be restricted.

Despite such developments, not all Brexit-supporting conservatives are poor. As Table 3.1 shows, 43 per cent of AB voters supported Brexit, many of whom are traditional conservatives. Though these citizens prefer the economic libertarian measures discussed above, they tend to be culturally conservative. Many are patriotic, while some support causes such as the death penalty and fox hunting. These traditional attitudes are based on resistance to change, evoking the Burkean argument that change upsets stability. In the parliamentary Conservative Party, figures such as Jacob Rees-Mogg are associated with this agenda. Certain conservatives are incorrigible traditionalists, echoing reactionary thinkers such as Donoso Cortés.[28]

Maintenance of the status quo is in the interests of the rich, lack of change preserving inequalities, yet traditional conservativism cannot be reduced to mere defence of privilege. As I explain above, ideas have a life of their own; conservative thought draws from numerous influences and has a long history. Conservatism has also taken a historically contingent path, reflecting past challenges. In the British case, the status of the country as an island is significant, meaning that conservatives value independence and a small state.[29]

Support of richer conservatives for Brexit can be explained in these terms. Brexit was in the material interests of certain wealthier conservatives, for example small businessowners who wished to evade European regulations,[30] yet in many cases attachment to conservative ideas was more significant. Other conservatives may have advocated Remain, yet one end point of a worldview which defended tradition was support for Brexit; this was particularly so in rural areas,[31] in which tradition is more important. British history also meant that sovereignty was crucial; this was a stronger argument of the Leave campaign.

Despite this legacy, I find it more difficult to explain richer conservative support for Brexit. As I emphasize in other parts of this book, EU membership is in the interests of the wealthier; this is true across Europe and, in the British case, is demonstrated by polls which show that rich citizens and larger businesses tended to support Remain.[32] Brexit also conflicts with conservative principles such as economic competence and aversion to change; I better understand support for Brexit among poor national populists. A wealthy Leave-voting friend chides me for Europhilia, suggesting that my own views make me unable to see flaws in the European project. There may be truth in this; we are all constrained by our sympathies. My framework also focuses on economic motives, characteristic of institutional theory, meaning that it is difficult to accept ideas in their own terms; philosophical approaches are better at this. Materialist explanations struggle with other facts about conservatism. Certain studies show that conservatism is associated with fear of death, this anxiety entailing preference for order.[33] No single approach can explain conservative views, yet such findings indicate the need to appreciate diverse influences. I will not pretend that I can explain correspondence between the politics and interests of all groups, much less those of individual citizens.

Conservatives admittedly contest arguments which have been made in this chapter, proposing various means of managing inequality. More felicitously, conservatives advocate philanthropy; more ominously, conservatives advocate authoritarian law and order methods. Though such approaches have successes, often in contexts in which alternatives are unfeasible, I am sceptical. Lavish cultures of philanthropy have coexisted with gross inequalities, studies finding that income inequality is associated with charity, while draconian law enforcement tends to be ineffective.[34] These debates are well-rehearsed and conservatives have established positions, yet recent experiences suggest that conservatism requires a basic rethink. In the years since the economic crisis, there is increasing consensus that deregulation causes serious problems; declining popularity among publics is notable.[35]

Conservatism is thus characterized by considerable externalization; because of the disruptive effects of conservative economic policies, the stability which is desired by conservatives is difficult to maintain. This problem may have been less acute historically, post-war conservatives rejecting economic libertarianism for measures which promoted stability, yet globalization has disrupted this balance. Not only has the process encouraged deregulation, but it quickens the spread of disorder. Because of these developments, economic and non-economic aspects of conservatism have conflicted with one another, causing a crisis of the worldview.

The tendency of conservatism to create externalization may be considerable, yet certain worldviews are worse. National populism is one; because of its propensity to create enemies, this position causes internal and external instability. Increasing overlap between conservatism and national populism is not coincidental. As the inability of conservatism to stem change has become evident, certain conservatives have become attracted to uncompromising stances.[36] Given this overlap, it is to national populism that I now turn.

Notes

1 Milton Friedman (1970) 'Interview in The Donahue Show'. Available at: https://interviews.televisionacademy.com/ interviews/phil-donahue. Accessed 17 May 2020.

2 Support bases of conservative parties are discussed by Daniel Oesch (2008) 'The Changing Shape of Class Voting: An Individual-Level Analysis of Party Support in Britain, Germany and Switzerland', *European Societies*, 10:3, 329–55.

3 The nature of support for the modern Conservative Party is evaluated by Tim Bale (2016) *The Conservative Party: From Thatcher to Cameron*. Cambridge: Polity Press. Recent preferences of low-income voters are assessed by Oliver Heath and Matthew Goodwin (2019) 'Low-Income Voters in UK General Elections, 1987–2017', Joseph Rowntree Foundation. Available at: www.jrf.org.uk/report/low-income-voters-uk-general-elections-1987-2017. Accessed 17 May 2020.

4 Definitional issues are discussed by Andrew Gamble (2013) 'Economic Libertarianism', in M. Freeden, L. T. Sargent and M. Stears (eds), *The Oxford Handbook of Political Ideologies*. Oxford: Oxford University Press, 405–21, and

Noel O'Sullivan (2013) 'Conservatism', in M. Freeden, L. T. Sargent and M. Stears (eds), *The Oxford Handbook of Political Ideologies*. Oxford: Oxford University Press, 293–311.

5 The economic and cultural basis of conservative support is assessed by Hanspeter Kriesi, Edgar Grande, Romain Lachat, Martin Dolezal, Simon Bornschier and Timotheos Frey (2008) *West European Politics in the Age of Globalization*. Cambridge: Cambridge University Press; Oesch, 'Changing Shape'.

6 Vivien A. Schmidt (2008) 'Discursive Institutionalism: The Explanatory Power of Ideas and Discourse', *Annual Review of Political Science*, 11:1, 303–26.

7 See Adam Smith (2010) *The Wealth of Nations: An Inquiry into the Nature and Causes of the Wealth of Nations*. Petersfield: Harriman House Limited; Friedrich Hayek (2014) *The Road to Serfdom: Text and Documents: The Definitive Edition*. London: Routledge; Milton Friedman, Leonard J. Savage and Gary S. Becker (2007) *Milton Friedman on Economics: Selected Papers*. Chicago: University of Chicago Press. Though such figures did not necessarily identify as conservatives, their ideas are crucial to the conservative canon.

8 Geraint Parry, George Moyser and Neil Day (1992) *Political Participation and Democracy in Britain*. Cambridge: Cambridge University Press.

9 Conservatism and the national interest is discussed by Jose Harris (2017) 'Principles, Markets and National Interest in Conservative Approaches to Social Policy', in C. Berthezène and J.-C. Vinel (eds), *Postwar Conservatism: A Transnational Investigation*. London: Palgrave Macmillan, 95–118.

10 This position is vividly articulated in the media, e.g. Owen Jones (2012) 'The Tories Do Have Policies: They Just Don't Want You to Know What They Are', *Guardian*. Available at: www.theguardian.com/commentisfree/2019/dec/05/the-tories-do-have-policies-they-just-dont-want-you-to-know-what-they-are. Accessed 17 May 2020; Gary Younge (2010) 'I Hate Tories. And Yes, It's Tribal', *Guardian*. Available at: www.theguardian.com/commentisfree/2010/may/04/why-i-hate-tories-david-cameron. Accessed 17 May 2020.

11 This term, which I use to frame discussions throughout this book, is my own. I am unaware of usage like mine, yet externalization is used to discuss field-specific phenomena in disciplines such as economics and psychology, e.g. Alison Davis-Blake and Brian Uzzi (1993) 'Determinants of Employment Externalization: A Study of Temporary Workers and Independent Contractors', *Administrative Science Quarterly*, 38:2, 195–223; Joseph Sandler and Meir Perlow (2018) 'Internalization and Externalization', in J. Sandler (ed.), *Projection, Identification, Projective Identification*. London: Routledge, 1–11.

12 Feargal McGuiness and Daniel Harari (2019) 'Income Inequality in the UK', UK Government Report. Available at: www.researchbriefings.files.parliament.uk/documents/CBP-7484/CBP-7484.pdf. Accessed 17 May 2020.

13 Robert Joyce, Thomas Pope and Barra Roantree (2019) 'The Characteristics and Incomes of the Top 1%', Institute for Fiscal Studies. Available at: www.ifs.org.uk/publications/14303. Accessed 17 May 2020.

14 Roger Eatwell and Matthew Goodwin (2018) *National Populism: The Revolt against Liberal Democracy.* London: Pelican.

15 There is extensive literature on inequality, e.g. Branko Milanovic (2016) *Global Inequality: A New Approach for the Age of Globalization*. Cambridge, MA: Harvard University Press; Thomas Piketty (2014) *Capital in the Twenty-First Century*. Cambridge, MA: Harvard University Press.

16 There is a useful review of existing literature in Kate E. Pickett and Richard G. Wilkinson (2015) 'Income Inequality and Health: A Causal Review', *Social Science & Medicine*, 128:2, 316–26. Though suicide is an exception, studies of diverse contexts have found that phenomena such as infant mortality, life expectancy and mental illness are related to inequality, Brian Biggs, Lawrence King, Sanjay Basu and David Stuckler (2010) 'Is Wealthier Always Healthier? The Impact of National Income Level, Inequality, and Poverty on Public Health in Latin America', *Social Science & Medicine*, 71:2, 266–73; Jonathan K. Burns, Andrew Tomita and Amy S. Kapadia (2014) 'Income Inequality

and Schizophrenia: Increased Schizophrenia Incidence in Countries with High Levels of Income Inequality', *International Journal of Social Psychiatry*, 60:2, 185–96; Michael Marmot and Martin Bobak (2000) 'International Comparators and Poverty and Health in Europe', *British Medical Journal*, 321:1, 11–24.

17 Research finds a persistent link between economic inequality and homicide, Maria D. H. Koeppel, Gayle M. Rhineberger-Dunn and Kristen Y. Mack (2015) 'Cross-National Homicide: A Review of the Current Literature', *International Journal of Comparative and Applied Criminal Justice*, 39:1, 47–85.

18 Edmund Burke (1986) *Reflections on the Revolution in France (1790)*. Oxford: Oxford University Press.

19 Karl Polanyi (1994) *The Great Transformation*. New York: Farrar & Rinehart.

20 Christoph Lakner and Branko Milanovic (2016) 'Global Income Distribution: From the Fall of the Berlin Wall to the Great Recession', *World Bank Economic Review*, 30:2, 203–32.

21 Rui Costa and Stephen Machin (2017) 'Real Wages and Living Standards in the UK'. Available from: http://cep.lse.ac.uk/pubs/download/ea036.pdf. Accessed 19 January 2020.

22 McGuiness and Harari, 'Income Inequality'.

23 Lakner and Milanovic, 'Global Income Distribution'.

24 Walter Garrison Runciman (1996) *Relative Deprivation and Social Justice: A Study of Attitudes to Social Inequality in Twentieth-Century England* (Vol. 13). Berkeley: University of California Press. There is now developed scholarship on relative deprivation, some of which links relative deprivation and conservative economic policies, e.g. Nemanja Džuverovic (2013) 'Does More (or Less) Lead to Violence? Application of the Relative Deprivation Hypothesis on Economic Inequality-Induced Conflicts', *Croatian International Relations Review*, 19:68, 53–72.

25 Justin Gest, Tyler Reny and Jeremy Mayer (2018) 'Roots of the Radical Right: Nostalgic Deprivation in the United States and Britain', *Comparative Political Studies*, 51:1, 1694–98; Matthijs Rooduijn and Brian Burgoon (2018) 'The

Paradox of Wellbeing: Do Unfavourable Socioeconomic and Sociocultural Contexts Deepen or Dampen Radical Left and Right Voting among the Less Well-Off?', *Comparative Political Studies*, 51:13, 1720–53.

26 Jan-Werner Müller (2016) *What is Populism?* Philadelphia: University of Pennsylvania Press.

27 Post-Brexit tensions in conservatism are discussed by Richard Hayton (2018) 'British Conservatism after the Vote for Brexit: The Ideological Legacy of David Cameron', *The British Journal of Politics and International Relations*, 20:1, 223–38.

28 O'Sullivan, 'Conservatism'.

29 Robert Eccleshall (2002) *English Conservatism since the Restoration: An Introduction and Anthology*. London: Routledge.

30 Brad MacKay (2016) 'Does Business Really Support "Remain" in the EU Referendum Debate?'. Business Views on the EU Referendum. Media Briefing, Centre on Constitutional Change, University of St Andrews, 20. Available at: www. centreonconstitutionalchange.ac.uk/sites/default/files/ migrated/papers/Business%20Surveys%20EU%20 Referendum_210616.pdf. Accessed 9 February 2020.

31 Will Jennings, Gerry Stoker and Ian Warren (2019) 'Cities and Towns: The Geography of Discontent', in *Brexit and Public Opinion 2019 UK in a Changing Europe*. Available at: www. ukandeu.ac.uk/wp-content/uploads/2019/01/Public-opinion-2019.pdf. Accessed 17 May 2020.

32 Wealth and support for European integration are linked by Matthew Gabel and Harvey Palmer (1995) 'Understanding Variation in Public Support for European Integration', *European Journal of Political Research*, 27:1, 3–19. Researching the Brexit referendum, similar findings are made by Sara B. Hobolt (2016) 'The Brexit Vote: A Divided Nation, a Divided Continent', *Journal of European Public Policy*, 23:9, 1259–77 and MacKay, 'Does Business Really Support "Remain"?'.

33 John T. Jost, Gráinne Fitzsimons and Aaron C. Kay (2004) 'The Ideological Animal: A System Justification View'. In J. Greenberg, S. L. Koole and T. A. Pyszczynski (eds), *Handbook of Experimental Existential Psychology*.

New York: Guilford Press, 263–82; Glenn D. Wilson (1973) *The Psychology of Conservatism*. London: Academic Press.

34 An association between inequality and charity is found by Giuseppe Mastromatteo and Francesco Flaviano Russo (2017) 'Inequality and Charity', *World Development*, 96:1, 136–44. Studies show limited deterrence effects of longer sentences and capital punishment, John M. Darley (2005) 'On the Unlikely Prospect of Reducing Crime Rates by Increasing the Severity of Prison Sentences', *Journal of Law and Policy*, 13:1, 189–208; Michael Radelet and Ronald L. Akers (1996) 'Deterrence and the Death Penalty: The Views of the Experts', *The Journal of Criminal Law and Criminology*, 87:1, 1–16.

35 British Social Attitudes 35 shows increasing preference for interventionism, Nancy Kelley, Christopher Warhurst and Robert Wishart (2018) 'Work and Welfare: The Changing Face of the UK Labour Market', in D. Phillips, J. Curtice, M. Phillips and J. Perry (eds), *British Social Attitudes: The 35th Report*. London: The National Centre for Social Research.

36 Paul Webb and Tim Bale (2014) 'Why Do Tories Defect to UKIP? Conservative Party Members and the Temptations of the Populist Radical Right', *Political Studies*, 62:4, 961–70.

Chapter 3

Are Brexiters stupid?

I had this sort of weird sense of unreality walking around [Ebbw Vale] and it came to a head when I met this young man in front of the [EU funded] sports centre. And he told me that he had voted to leave because the European Union had done nothing for him ... All around town people told me the same thing; they said that they wanted to take back control ... They told me that they were most fed up with the immigrants and with the refugees ... When I checked the figures, I discovered that Ebbw Vale actually has one of the lowest rates of immigration in the country. (Carole Cadwalladr)[1]

The best they can expect from the future is the return of the old order, from which they expect the restoration of their social being. (Pierre Bourdieu)[2]

National populism[3] is a worldview of our times. In recent years, following the disruptive effects of glo-balization, politicians such as Donald Trump, Nigel Farage and Marine Le Pen have achieved widespread appeal. National populists blame others for the ills of the common person. Groups which are held responsible differ from country to country, yet common targets include immigrants, the EU and Roma. British national populists such as UKIP and the Brexit Party have experienced uneven support, yet the Brexit vote means that national populism is increasingly espoused by the Conservative Party. Britain is far from alone. On the continent, various movements threaten the stability of the EU, among them the German Alternative for Germany and French Rassemblement National,[4] while the election of Donald Trump represented a political earthquake.

The case of national populism offers a fascinating insight into the relationship between self-interest and politics. In the aftermath of the Brexit vote, the fact that many areas which benefited from EU funding had voted Leave attracted attention. Ebbw Vale, a former mining town in the Welsh Valleys, was a celebrated case; European money had been lavished on it, financing multimillion investments in transport and further education, yet 62 per cent[5] of voters supported Leave.[6] There are similar cases in other countries. Many are bewildered that Donald Trump, a politician with strong ties to big business, could attract the votes of blue-collar workers. Yet this phenomenon is long-standing. For many years, Marxists have regretted the propensity of workers to back movements which are considered counter to their real interests, workers who prefer conservatives provoking particular bemusement.[7]

Table 3.1   Brexit referendum voting by social grade[1]

Social grade	Remain	Leave
AB (Higher and intermediate managerial, administrative or professional)	56.9%	43.1%
C1 (Supervisory or clerical and junior managerial, administrative or professional)	54.1%	45.9%
C2 (Skilled manual workers)	40.3%	59.7%
DE (Semi-skilled and unskilled manual workers, state pensioners, casual and lowest grade workers, unemployed with state benefits only)	40.1%	59.7%

Source: British Election Study.

[1] The National Readership Survey (NRS) identifies six social grades; A (upper-middle class), B (middle class), C1 (lower-middle class), C2 (skilled working class), D (working class) and E (non-working).

Cases differ according to time and place, yet critiques underestimate the extent to which such worldviews fulfil the needs of low income and education voters. This is demonstrated by national populism, a position which satisfies the desire of such citizens for stability in a globalized world. Not all national-populist supporters are poor and not all poor are national-populist supporters (see Table 3.1). In the former case, rich national populists such as Donald Trump use such movements to advance business interests, some considering Trump an outright cynic.[8] In the latter case, factors including education and minority status make some poor citizens less likely to favour national populism.

Why Brexit benefits low income and education voters

National populism is attractive to low income and education voters for material and non-material reasons. The tendency of such movements to advocate redistributive policies is often forgotten. Though certain national populists are associated with free market measures promoted by conservatives, the most notable of whom is Donald Trump, many favour interventionist policies and regard free markets as corrosive to traditional ways of life. In areas such as housing and social security, the Brexit Party and Rassemblement National advocate redistributive measures. The Polish case is worthy of special mention. In this country, the national-populist Law and Justice (PiS) government has transformed society with policies which improve the position of the poorest; the flagship 500+ child benefit policy, which awards a monthly 500 złoty (approximately £100) for every child, is noteworthy.[9] Economic redistribution and cultural conservatism complement each another; for reasons of security, lower classes desire societies in which living conditions are decent but tradition prevails. Movements which combine these goals have been uncommon in Western countries, yet research suggests that this is anomalous; a study of ninety-nine countries found that it was more common for right-wing cultural views to be coupled with left-wing economic views, particularly among poorer citizens.[10] Increasing low-income support for the Conservative Party explains the Johnson government's adoption of certain redistributive measures, evident in the 2020 Budget.[11]

Although material factors help explain support for national populists, the case of national populism offers profound insight into the capacity of non-material factors to satisfy the needs of low income and education citizens. Non-material aspects of national populism are related to the socio-economic profile of national-populist supporters, the low mobility of such groups meaning that they favour preservation of local conditions. Emphasis on national identity also appeals to citizens with low individual status, offering psychological consolation.[12] These are major reasons for the success of national populism and demonstrate the conditions in which self-interest coalesces with non-material factors.

We live in an age which is more globalized than previous periods of history; flows of capital, goods and people between countries have significantly increased in recent decades. In this world, mobility is a key asset. The span of jobs has shortened and lucrative positions appear in diverse locations; mobility thus allows maximization of earnings. Communities in post-industrial areas such as the Welsh Valleys tend to be unable to take advantage of mobility. This is associated with lower skill profiles. Because of traditional reliance on disappearing manual jobs and the poor quality of public education, citizens in these areas often lack education and skills. Related issues, such as absence of relevant networks and poor confidence, further impede job searches away from communities. These are the 'somewhere' citizens described by David Goodhart, a category contrasted with educated and mobile 'any-wheres'. According to Goodhart, the embeddedness of somewheres in specific places means that they favour traditionalist policies in spheres such as immigration, vocational training and female employment.[13] Scholars note the importance of mobility under globalization. In a seminal work, Kriesi and colleagues emphasize *exit options*.[14] Because of their marketable skills, the educated can leave places when conditions deteriorate; the uneducated lack this ability.

The objection that immigrants from poorer countries find jobs in Britain is problematic. The skill profile of immigrants from countries such as Poland tends to be higher than citizens who remain; emigrants often have degrees and experience of foreign travel.[15] In countries which send immigrants, immobile citizens suffer inverse problems.[16] I once conducted research on working conditions in Polish hospitals and was shocked to discover that Polish nurses have an average age of 50;[17] this is related to emigration and worsens the quality of Polish healthcare.

Because they have limited exit options, those who live in communities such as Ebbw Vale have an interest in cultivating long-term relationships with localities. Work is an obvious case. Given that such citizens have less ability to find jobs elsewhere, secure local employment is crucial. Social and cultural activities play a complementary role. Institutions such as rugby clubs, choirs and churches, historically pillars of towns such as Ebbw Vale, create important spaces for citizens to solidify bonds with localities. In short, local people have high levels of personal capital in such communities.[18] Quite aside from economic livelihoods, networks of family and friends reside in these places. Comparisons with rich urban communities are instructive. Because of a greater ability to find work in other places, coupled with looser links to the communities in which they reside, the personal capital of the wealthier is less tied up in single localities. Residents would be inconvenienced if conditions in Hampstead were to deteriorate, yet most would relocate without great difficulty; this is not the case in places such as Ebbw Vale.

When capital is bound up in one place, change is particularly threatening. This has always been the case, such communities historically resisting restructuring, yet globalization means that sensitivities are more often piqued; this process involves heightened change. Developments in recent decades scarcely inspire confidence. In this time, the economies of places like Ebbw Vale have been ravaged by deindustrialization; this has led to a steep decline in the blue-collar jobs which sustained economies and gave residents, particularly men, a sense of identity. Civil society has also decayed. As society has become more individual, institutions such as rugby clubs and choirs have undergone declines in membership. Scholars recognize the dangers of this. In *Bowling Alone*, the political scientist Robert Putnam emphasized the decline of civil society in the United States, arguing that the process imperilled democracy; if citizens associated less, they were deprived of the political conversations upon which healthy democracies depend.[19]

Many post-industrial areas have been affected by a particularly threatening form of change: mass migration. The capacity of migration to transform the character of communities makes it particularly disquieting. For many decades, incoming migrants have tended to settle in low-income areas; they have often done so in considerable numbers, forming separate communities which are culturally distinct from the existing population. In Britain, there are egregious cases in northern mill towns such as Bradford and Burnley; these places are unrecognizable from the tight-knit communities of previous decades.

Such processes are threatening to residents. There are certain material issues. Though research shows that recent immigration has tended not to affect public services, high employment rates of migrants ensuring a net fiscal contribution,[20] the implications for wages are more ambiguous. Effects on average wages are small, yet poorer citizens are more exposed to negative impacts.[21] One study of the British labour market found that immigration depressed wages of the lowest paid, though led to slight increases for the highest paid;[22] another discovered that immigration has a small negative effect on average British wages, most pronounced within the semi/unskilled services occupational group.[23] At the very least, it is difficult to conclude that mass migration improves the relative position of working classes.

Economic concerns may not always motivate anti-immigrant attitudes, studies showing that authoritarian values are often more important,[24] yet unfavourable changes create conditions in which discontent emerges. Negative marginal changes are crucial; as emphasized in Chapter 2, they pique sensitivities disproportionately. In non-material terms, segregation undermines the cohesion which is so valuable in low-income communities. This would be disconcerting enough for mobile citizens. When it occurs in places with immobile populations, the effects can be traumatic. This is compounded by disruption to ethnic hierarchies, the loss of relative status provoking resentment.[25] Beyond these considerations, the prospect of future immigration, which could further disturb local conditions, poses a psychological threat; this is heightened in a globalized world.

It is easy to see how scepticism towards globalization takes root in this soil. Because such communities have most to fear from change and previous changes have been harmful, a backlash against globalization takes place. European investments in a town such as Ebbw Vale, even when spent on projects which improve conditions, were comparatively insignificant. Long-term decline had taken place, linked to globalization; a vote for Brexit was a means of potentially slowing these changes and such populations grasped it. Many

considered this foolish.[26] Quite aside from the economic implications of Brexit, which may affect such
communities severely, there are implications in the
international sphere; as I argue below, the tendency of
national populism to increase external tension means
that the worldview can damage the common good.

Despite these caveats, many aspects of Brexit were
consistent with the interests of low income and education citizens; Brexit had the potential to slow flows of
people and capital and assert popular control over globalization. Crucially, the comparative position of those
who supported Brexit was poor. Change had bitten into
communities for many decades, leaving places shells
of their former selves; major ground had been lost to
the mobile. Though assertions that such citizens had
'nothing to lose'[27] are untrue, one has only to think of
conditions in the developing world, lashing out against
the establishment was not irrational. Given the poor
relative position of these groups, a reordering of the
system was potentially advantageous. It is paradoxical
that immobility underpinned this. In different conditions, attachment to place makes humans risk-averse;
one survey found that, among Leave voters, the poorer
were more worried by a no deal outcome.[28] Gambles
with change are nonetheless a hallmark of national
populism. When ways of life are under threat, voters
rebel against establishments in the hope of achieving
systemic changes.

In the case of Ebbw Vale, another debated issue was
the lack of immigrants; pre-Brexit immigration into

Ebbw Vale was low and the ethnic composition of the town is overwhelmingly white. In that it expressed opposition to immigration while having few immigrants, Ebbw Vale was not unique; other areas which supported Brexit had similar demographic profiles. Though critics seized upon this as evidence of the misguided actions of voters, this view is also problematic. As Eatwell and Goodwin emphasize, support for Brexit was stronger in areas which experienced higher rates of immigration, rather than areas which are ethnically diverse.[29] Concerns also anticipate future immigration. As I have stressed, there are good reasons for considering immigration to lie in tension with the interests of low income and education communities. Given that towns such as Ebbw Vale are integrated with the rest of the country through a common political system and media, trends in other localities are highly relevant; they demonstrate future trajectories. Developments in many places were unattractive to residents of Ebbw Vale, who considered immigration to have undermined cohesion.

This shows how ideas spread. Once positions become established among classes of people, often reflecting overall preferences, the ideas themselves achieve an influence which can override individual realities. Residents of Ebbw Vale may have seldom encountered immigrants themselves, yet the prevalence of anti-immigrant views among their social class meant that these ideas were influential. Research confirms that national-populist ideas diffuse indirectly. Economic decline is not always the cause of support for national populists, studies finding an unconvincing link with unemployment and relative deprivation.[30] Links between mobility and national-populist views are also contingent, one study showing that individuals who are more involved in civic organizations are *less* pro-Brexit.[31] Despite these qualifications, national populism has a genuine basis. Scholarship on exit options shows the structural foundations of the worldview,[32] while recent studies emphasize economic causes, finding that national populism reflects individual hardship in prosperous overall contexts.[33] This is consistent with the sociology of knowledge, explained in Chapter 4, which sees ideas as products of social status.[34]

Ideas diffuse by several means. Within countries, certain institutions are common to specific classes; these include newspapers, political parties and social media habits. In a symbiotic process, ideas which are in the general class interest spread through these institutions, incrementally obtaining hegemony. In the British case, tabloid presses have been major diffusers of working-class opinion, articulating key demands. There are examples of this process among other classes. In cases in which wealthier citizens work in sectors which would be favoured by Brexit, for example managers in the fishing industry, wider class influences are likely more significant. In Chapter 4, I examine the means by which certain ideas predominate.

My argument that tabloid presses articulate genuine lower-class opinions will be controversial. On the left, there are developed critiques of publications like the *Sun*, detractors regarding such newspapers as stirring prejudices to distract from wider inequalities. This view is associated with a broader critique of national populism. Rather than representing authentic interests of low-income groups, national populism is thought to distort the real interests of such citizens. The Marxist theory of false consciousness embodies this, asserting that non-progressive views of working classes reflect the manipulative influence of capital.[35] Aside from Marxists, many were quick to point out the spurious grounds on which Brexit supporters voted; we all heard of Leave supporters who wished to refight the war or avenge Eurovision defeats. Though researchers tend not to credit direct processes of manipulation, the influence of education is well-attested; studies show that it predicts liberal values better than occupation.[36] In a classic work, Lipset noted that the lower sophistication of the less educated meant that they interpreted politics in black-and-white terms, making them prone to support extremists; Norris and Inglehart suggest that this concern remains relevant.[37]

Tempting as it may be to dismiss national populism as the cry of fools, this is problematic. In the case of Brexit, there is research which suggests that Leave and Remain voters had equivalent knowledge of the EU; a study which asked a representative sample fifteen questions about the EU found there was no average difference in knowledge between the groups.[38] More broadly, national populism has spiked in almost all

Western countries; these contexts are diverse and many lack illiberal tabloid presses. This suggests that the worldview has a function.

Appreciation of national-populist values helps us understand this function. The work of psychologist Jonathan Haidt, which identifies five moral foundations (care, fairness, loyalty, authority and sanctity), shows the importance of loyalty and authority to national populists.[39] Though liberals and left-wingers are inspired by altruism, Haidt demonstrating their concern with care and fairness, it would be unfair to suggest that national populists are not altruistic. The success of campaigns such as Help for Heroes, which raises money for injured soldiers and is supported by national populists, shows that this is not the case. Just as altruistic acts of liberals are often performed in service of liberal causes, support for refugees for example, national-populist altruism is associated with values such as patriotism.

In a changing world, such values satisfy desires for security. Because globalization tends to disadvantage national-populist supporters, inspiring feelings of shame associated with low status and relative deprivation,[40] these voters favour worldviews which reassert traditional identities. Given weakness of individual identities, this is understandable. *Take back control* tapped into this, evoking times when Britain ran an empire and immigration was low. Aside from socioeconomic functions, slowing parts of globalization which threaten immobile citizens, national populism fulfils emotional purposes; it boosts the confidence of supporters, many of whom feel misunderstood by political classes. The remarks of my mother-in-law, a Polish small farmer with little formal education who supports the national-populist PiS government, are revelatory. Although she tells us that she has difficulty understanding liberal politicians, cultivated Warsaw elites, she perfectly understands Jarosław Kaczyński, PiS leader and Trump model. Such politicians might be rich, as are Trump and Johnson, yet their earthy styles attract the disadvantaged; appeals to national and religious pride are especially potent. When these figures assume office, supporter morale improves.

Given such considerations, the most reasonable conclusion is that national populism is in the interests of certain low income and education voters. This interpretation is more parsimonious than others and avoids patronising national-populist supporters. I would also emphasize the millions who support national populism, implying that idiosyncrasies subside, and the cross-country appeal of the worldview. Institutions such as tabloid presses may well sometimes function as agents of the rich, influencing readers in nefarious ways, yet such forces cannot explain major increases in support for national populism. There are important exceptions among low-income groups. Ethnic minorities disproportionately reject national populism,[41] because of its discriminatory basis. Age is also relevant, younger low-income citizens being less likely to favour national populism than older counterparts. This is related to better educational attainment, though also reflects postmaterial values.[42]

There are cases in which national-populist ideas appear severely at odds with the interests of supporters. In recent years, lower-class national populists have hoped for a no deal Brexit, despite indication that poorer citizens would be most impacted by this outcome. There are time-scale issues, national populists asserting that the long-term benefits of Brexit would be worth short-term injury, yet such cases demonstrate the conditional relationship between ideas and self-interest. Worldviews have separate parts, reflecting peculiar developmental paths. Though most elements may be consistent with the interests of supporters, certain aspects can lie in tension. Historic links between Euroscepticism and national populism ensured that Brexit obtained its own momentum, meaning that lower-class national populists supported damaging actions. In a study of nationalism, Varshney distinguishes between 'instrumental rationality' and 'value rationality'.[43] The former involves strict cost–benefit calculus, whereas the latter entails dedication to values and can include personal sacrifice. Commitment to no deal Brexit is not the most extreme form of value rationality, such behaviour including religious martyrdom, yet is on this spectrum; it subordinates material interests to ideology.

Such problems have no definitive answer. National populism can reflect the authentic interests of lower classes *and* the distortive influence of capital, the two influences coexisting. In certain contexts, the hand of business appears more powerful; this is the case with the Trump presidency, characterized by strong links with large firms and pro-business policies. I find lower-class Trump supporters more difficult to explain. In other settings, business influence is less potent and advantages for lower classes are more obvious. Aside from the Polish case, the Brexit Party and Rassemblement National advocate generous social policies.

We are also at an early stage of understanding. Though multiple studies have been published, the recent appearance of the phenomenon means that there are limits to comprehension. Such caveats are vital, yet the relationship between national populism and lower-class interests remains apparent; the least that can be said is that many commentators underplay this.

Why national populism is dangerous

Despite its capacity to satisfy certain needs of low income and education voters, national populism is associated with damaging forms of externalization. There are several which might be listed, environmentalists baulking at the damage such movements are prepared to inflict on the planet, but the potential of national populists to cause conflict is particularly notable. This results from the tendency of national populism to create enemies. There is little intrinsic in the desire to preserve local conditions which makes this inevitable – in many countries there are agricultural parties which, though placing emphasis on tradition, reject extremism – yet this is a key feature of national populism.[44]

National populists identify internal and external enemies. These 'others' differ according to national context,[45] yet are typically minorities. In Britain, immigrants and Muslims are stigmatized. Such enemies allow national populists to blame others for the hardships of supporters, a process encouraged by the difficult conditions in which many national-populist voters live. Even if such scapegoating cannot be directly linked to self-interest, it is associated with movements which harness popular impetus in defence of local conditions. Such energy requires targets, which marginalized groups provide. This is nonetheless dangerous for society as a whole; it creates instability, ultimately threatening the good of all, including national populists.

Scapegoating causes internal unrest. Even when national populists are not in power, derogatory language creates pressure for measures which penalize 'others'; recent Conservative governments, which have sought to appease UKIP and Brexit Party voters through punitive immigration policies, are a classic case and examples exist on the continent.[46] When national populists are in power, such tendencies are even more marked. Though some national-populist complaints have roots in reality, abuses associated with immigration and welfare being undeniable, policies which penalize minorities tend to create conflict.

As one would expect, targeted groups respond negatively to such measures. From Roma victimized by the Hungarian government to Muslims harassed by Front National inspired policies in France, unrest foments among such groups. This is expressed in more innocuous forms such as distrust of the government, which is nonetheless corrosive, and highly damaging acts such as terrorism; in the French case, government mistreatment of minorities has contributed to the series of attacks endured by the country, even if other factors are significant. National populists typically react to such developments with intensified scapegoating. Minorities may sometimes not be blameless, yet aggression towards them is counterproductive; it creates vicious circles, inflaming situations and escalating the risk of further disorder.

Internal conflict is damaging enough, yet a related development is more concerning; this is the potential of national populism to create external conflict.[47] As the case of 1930s Europe shows, governments which excite national sentiment often conflict with neighbours. We may note links with internal unrest. In these years, the creation of 'others' such as Jews and Slavs encouraged conflict with neighbours; this resulted not only from the energy for aggressive foreign policies which these campaigns created, but also from deteriorating relations with states which protected such minorities. The escalation of these cycles should remind us of the dangers.

It is true that history never repeats itself. Contemporary national populists are less extreme than older counterparts, a few exceptions notwithstanding. Such movements are also yet to cause serious conflict. This nonetheless reflects the fact that national populists are largely excluded from government. If one reviews the programmes of these parties, worrying precedents are evident. Particularly concerning are national-populist attitudes to Western alliances.[48] Even if they are not perfect, the EU and NATO have guaranteed European peace for over seventy years. This is associated with structural changes introduced by these organizations. Following the end of the Second World War, itself a coda to centuries of European conflict, NATO and the European Communities recast Europe in a way conducive to harmony between countries. Given the long period of peace since their creation, it is difficult to deny that this goal has been achieved. At their best, such organizations reconcile separate domestic and international interests.[49]

National-populist programmes are troubling because they attempt to undo these institutions. The unravelling of NATO and the EU might not guarantee war in Europe, factors such as nuclear proliferation also accounting for global declines in armed conflict,[50] yet would represent an alarming development. This is particularly the case given the international order preferred by national populists. In place of liberal multilateralism, national populists advocate a Europe of nation states, in which ethnic majorities dominate; Jean-Marie Le Pen spoke of a Europe of homelands.

Such a world would not necessarily be conflict-prone. National-populist preference for isolationism and tight borders has its appeal. In recent decades, liberal interventionism has been associated with conflict.[51] Though some actions were defensible, such as Kosovo, others were not, such as Iraq. The Trump presidency has also been relatively pacific. Despite these concessions, we should worry about a national-populist world order. A Europe of nation states would not only codify competition between countries, but would encourage internal and external othering. The benefits of isolation are likely illusory. In an influential essay, international relations scholar Stephen Van Evera emphasizes the dangers of isolationism. Because of reduced penalties for expansion, associated with the retreat of dominant powers, isolationism makes conflict more probable; Van Evera notes that British and American isolation encouraged continental war.[52] Strengthened links with Russia, a desire of most national populists, are scarcely more appealing. Not only is the Russia of Vladimir Putin a revisionist power, annexing Crimea, but it is a sponsor of the illiberal policies which cause international tension. We must also remember that disorder is an explicit goal of Putin; a divided Europe benefits Russia. National-populist association with this aim will scarcely reassure those fearful of the movement.

Rather than peaceably reconciling different interests, national populism thus involves the belligerent assertion of a particular interest, potentially jeopardizing the welfare of all. Its reaction to globalization is disproportionate. Recent changes have disadvantaged national-populist supporters, yet the tendency of national populism to cause internal and external conflict threatens the common good. This is particularly the case in a globalized world which, for better or worse, is highly interconnected. Brexit must be seen in this context. Rupturing relations with allies on the continent, it is difficult to see how the process could not increase tensions with other European countries; Brexit negotiations, involving standoffs with the EU, are evidence of this. Even if Brexit does not involve war with European partners, it escalates tension and increases the probability of later conflict. This is part of the structural weakening of multilateral institutions, the dangers of which I have outlined.

There is admitted tension in my analysis of consequences of national populism; critics will notice that I am more relaxed about internal repercussions, involving the protection of localities from outsiders, than implications in the international sphere. I would emphasize the seriousness of outcomes. The tightening of borders rightly raises concerns, yet is less grave an outcome than conflict between countries. If my argument is followed, the former may also make the latter less likely. Liberalism, emphasizing links between internal and external liberties, is an alternative to national populism; I now consider this worldview.

Notes

1 Carole Cadwalladr (2019) 'Facebook's Role in Brexit and the Threat to Democracy', TED Talk. Available at: www.ted.com/talks/carole_cadwalladr_facebook_s_role_in_brexit_and_the_threat_to_democracy#t-161574. Accessed 17 May 2020.

2 Pierre Bourdieu (1984) *Distinction: A Social Critique of the Judgement of Taste*. Cambridge, MA: Harvard University Press, 111.

3 I avoid pejorative terms and worried about use of the word 'populism'. Despite this concern, lack of alternative terms means that 'national populism' is most appropriate. 'Nativism' involves hostility to foreign influences and 'nationalism' is associated with external belligerence, yet neither capture the internal and external attitudes which interest me. 'National populism' is established in literature, Eatwell and Goodwin using it. Populism involves anti-elitism and preference for direct participation, studied movements adopting these stances, see Jan-Werner Müller (2016) *What is Populism?* Philadelphia: University of Pennsylvania Press.

4 Known as Front National until June 2018.

5 This is the result for the Blaenau Gwent constituency. Specific data on Ebbw Vale are unavailable.

6 Cadwalladr's interpretation is instructive, Carole Cadwalladr (2016) 'Endless Lies Persuaded Ebbw Vale to Vote Leave', *Guardian*. Available at: www.theguardian.com/commentisfree/2016/jul/02/ebbw-vale-eu-vote-leave. Accessed 17 May 2020.

7 Ron Eyerman (1981) 'False Consciousness and Ideology in Marxist Theory', *Acta Sociologica*, 24:2, 43–56.

8 Gary Younge (2019) 'Trump's a Racist Conman – and that's the Brand America Bought', *Guardian*. Available at: www.theguardian.com/commentisfree/2019/feb/28/donald-trump-michael-cohen-racist-conman-america. Accessed 17 May 2020.

9 Thomas Prosser and Giga Giorgadze (2018) 'Towards a Theory of Illiberal Dualisation? Conceptualising New

Employment and Social Policy Divisions in Poland and the United Kingdom', *Transfer: European Review of Labour and Research*, 24:2, 151–62.

10 Ariel Malka, Yphtach Lelkes and Christopher J. Soto (2017) 'Are Cultural and Economic Conservatism Positively Correlated? A Large-Scale Cross-National Test', *British Journal of Political Science*, 49:3, 1–25.

11 Thomas Prosser (2020) 'Budget 2020: Why the Conservatives are Placing More Emphasis on Redistribution', LSE British Politics and Policy. Available at: https://blogs.lse.ac.uk/ politicsandpolicy/budget-2020-redistribution/. Accessed 17 May 2020.

12 Jens Rydgren (2003) 'Meso-Level Reasons for Racism and Xenophobia: Some Converging and Diverging Effects of Radical Right Populism in France and Sweden', *European Journal of Social Theory*, 6:1, 53–54; Jens Rydgren (2013) *Class Politics and the Radical Right*. London: Routledge, 9.

13 David Goodhart (2017) *The Road to Somewhere: The Populist Revolt and the Future of Politics*. London: C. Hurst & Co.

14 Hanspeter Kriesi, Edgar Grande, Romain Lachat, Martin Dolezal, Simon Bornschier and Timotheos Frey (2008) *West European Politics in the Age of Globalization*. Cambridge: Cambridge University Press, 5.

15 Christian Dustmann, Tommaso Frattini and Anna Rosso (2015) 'The Effect of Emigration from Poland on Polish Wages', *The Scandinavian Journal of Economics*, 117:2, 522–64, 523.

16 Atis Berzins and Peteris Zvidrins (2011) 'Depopulation in the Baltic States', *Lithuanian Journal of Statistics*, 50:1, 39–48.

17 Naczelna Izba Pielęgniarek i Położnych (2018) 'Raport Naczelnej Rady Pielęgniarek i Położnych: zabezpieczenie społeczeństwa polskiego w świadczenia pielęgniarek i położnych'. Available at: www.nipip.pl/wp-content/uploads/ 2017/03/Raport_druk_2017.pdf. Accessed 9 February 2020.

18 Social capital theory asserts the importance of social relationships, Nan Lin (2001) *Social Capital: A Theory of Social Structure and Action*. Cambridge: Cambridge University Press. There is literature on post-industrial areas, Cara

Aitchison and Tom Evans (2003) 'The Cultural Industries and a Model of Sustainable Regeneration: Manufacturing "Pop" in the Rhondda Valleys of South Wales', *Managing Leisure*, 8:3, 133–44; David Walsh, Gerry McCartney, Sarah McCullough, Marjon van der Pol, Duncan Buchanan and Russell Jones (2015) 'Comparing Levels of Social Capital in Three Northern Post-Industrial UK Cities', *Public Health*, 129:6, 629–38.

19 Robert D. Putnam (2000) *Bowling Alone: The Collapse and Revival of American Community*. New York: Simon & Schuster.

20 Oxford Economics (2018) 'The Fiscal Impact of Immigration on the UK'. Available at: www.oxfordeconomics.com/recent-releases/8747673d-3b26-439b-9693-0e250df6dbba. Accessed 1 February 2020.

21 Literature is discussed by Martin Ruhs and Carlos Vargas-Silva (2017) 'Briefing: The Labour Market Effects of Immigration'. The Migration Observatory. Available at: http://migrationobservatory.ox.ac.uk/wp-content/uploads/2016/04/Briefing-Labour_Market_Effects_Immigration.pdf. Accessed 17 May 2020.

22 Christian Dustmann, Tommaso Frattini and Ian P. Preston (2012) 'The Effect of Immigration Along the Distribution of Wages', *Review of Economic Studies*, 80:1, 145–73.

23 Stephen Nickell and Jumana Saleheen (2015) 'The Impact of Immigration on Occupational Wages: Evidence from Britain', Bank of England Working Paper 574.

24 David Card, Christian Dustmann and Ian Preston (2012) 'Immigration, Wages, and Compositional Amenities', *Journal of European Economic Association*, 10:1, 78–119; Jens Hainmueller and Michael J. Hiscox (2010) 'Attitudes toward Highly Skilled and Low-Skilled Immigration: Evidence from a Survey Experiment', *American Political Science Review*, 104:1, 61–84; Jens Hainmueller and Daniel J. Hopkins (2014) 'Public Attitudes toward Immigration', *Annual Review of Political Science*, 17:1, 225–49.

25 Arlie Russell Hochschild (2018) *Strangers in their Own Land: Anger and Mourning on the American Right*. New York: The New Press.

26 Cadwalladr, 'Endless Lies'.

27 Frances Ryan (2016) 'Martin's Already Lost Almost Everything: He Voted Leave to Spread the Pain', *Guardian*. Available at: www.theguardian.com/commentisfree/ 2016/jun/30/martin-nothing-lose-vote-leave-unemployed-benefits-sanctioned. Accessed 17 May 2020.

28 Uta Staiger, Christina Pagel and Christabel Cooper (2019) 'With No-Deal Now Leavers' Preferred Brexit Outcome, Ruling It Out Could Create Problems for the Tories'. Available at: www.huffingtonpost.co.uk/entry/no-deal-leavers_uk_5ca902dae4b0a00f6d408928. Accessed 17 May 2020.

29 Roger Eatwell and Matthew Goodwin (2018) *National Populism: The Revolt against Liberal Democracy*. London: Pelican, 165. There are similar findings in other European countries, e.g. Matt Golder (2003) 'Explaining Variation in the Success of Extreme Right Parties in Western Europe', *Comparative Political Studies*, 36:4, 432–66; Jens Rydgren and Patrick Ruth (2013) 'Contextual Explanations of Radical Right-Wing Support in Sweden: Socioeconomic Marginalization, Group Threat, and the Halo Effect', *Ethnic and Racial Studies*, 36:4, 711–28.

30 Marcel Lubbers, Mérove Gijsberts and Peer Scheepers (2002) 'Extreme Right-Wing Voting in Western Europe', *European Journal of Political Research*, 4:1, 345–78; Tim Spier (2010) *Modernisierungsverlierer? Die Wählerschaft rechtspopulistischer Parteien in Westeuropa*. Wiesbaden: VS Verlag für Sozialwissenschaften; Duane Swank and Hans-Georg Betz (2003) 'Globalization, the Welfare State and Right-Wing Populism in Western Europe', *Socio-Economic Review*, 1:2, 215–45.

31 Tak Wing Chan, Morag Henderson, Maria Sironi and Juta Kawalerowicz (2017) 'Understanding the Social and Cultural Bases of Brexit', Department of Quantitative Social Science, University College London, 17.

32 Kriesi et al., *West European Politics*, 5.

33 Matthijs Rooduijn and Brian Burgoon (2018) 'The Paradox of Wellbeing: Do Unfavourable Socioeconomic and Sociocultural Contexts Deepen or Dampen Radical Left

and Right Voting among the Less Well-Off?', *Comparative Political Studies*, 51:13, 1720–53.

34 Karl Mannheim (1960) *Ideology and Utopia: An Introduction to the Sociology of Knowledge*. London: Routledge.

35 Eyerman, 'False Consciousness'. Brexit is discussed in these terms by Paul Mason (2016) 'Brexit is a Fake Revolt: Working Class Culture is being Hijacked to Help the Elite', *Guardian*. Available at: www.theguardian.com/commentisfree/2016/jun/20/brexit-fake-revolt-eu-working-class-culture-hijacked-help-elite. Accessed 17 May 2020.

36 Pippa Norris and Ronald Inglehart (2019) *Cultural Backlash: Trump, Brexit, and Authoritarian Populism*. Cambridge: Cambridge University Press; Paula Surridge (2016) 'Education and Liberalism: Pursuing the Link', *Oxford Review of Education*, 42:2, 146–64; Herman G. Van de Werfhorst and Nan Dirk de Graaf (2004) 'The Sources of Political Orientations in Post-Industrial Society: Social Class and Education Revisited', *The British Journal of Sociology*, 55:2, 211–35.

37 Seymour Martin Lipset (1959) 'Democracy and Working-Class Authoritarianism', *American Sociological Review*, 24:4, 482–97; Norris and Inglehart, *Cultural Backlash*.

38 Noah Carl (2019) 'Are Leave Voters Less Knowledgeable about the EU than Remain Voters?'. Available at: www.ukandeu.ac.uk/are-leave-voters-less-knowledgeable-about-the-eu-than-remain-voters/. Accessed 19 January 2020.

39 Jonathan Haidt (2012) *The Righteous Mind: Why Good People are Divided by Politics and Religion*. New York: Random House.

40 Leonardo Carella and Robert Ford (2020) 'The Status Stratification of Radical Right Support: Reconsidering the Occupational Profile of UKIP's Electorate'. Available at: www.drive.google.com/file/d/1gGxz5EQHaaxoVE5Jmgn nW1WnyzbD7WeD/view. Accessed 17 May 2020.

41 Nicole Martin, Maria Sobolewska and Neema Begum (2019) 'Left Out of the Left Behind: Ethnic Minority Support for Brexit', Social Science Research Network.

42 Ronald Inglehart (1977) *The Silent Revolution: Changing Values and Political Styles among Western Publics*.

Princeton: Princeton University Press; Norris and Inglehart, *Cultural Backlash*.

43 Ashutosh Varshney (2003) 'Nationalism, Ethnic Conflict, and Rationality', *Perspectives on Politics*, 1:1, 85–99.

44 Hans-Georg Betz (2017) 'Nativism Across Time and Space', *Swiss Political Science Review*, 23:4, 335–53; Cristina C. Santamaría Graff (2017) ' "Build That Wall!": Manufacturing the Enemy, Yet Again', *International Journal of Qualitative Studies in Education*, 30:10, 999–1005.

45 Concerns of national movements are elaborated in Eatwell and Goodwin, *National Populism*.

46 Ferruh Yilmaz (2012) 'Right-Wing Hegemony and Immigration: How the Populist Far-Right Achieved Hegemony through the Immigration Debate in Europe', *Current Sociology*, 60:3, 368–81.

47 Though international relations scholars traditionally emphasize systemic influences, see Jervis, 'Realism, Neoliberalism, and Cooperation', there is increasing focus on domestic variables and the way they shape international outcomes, see Stephen Chaudoin, Helen V. Milner and Xun Pang (2015) 'International Systems and Domestic Politics: Linking Complex Interactions with Empirical Models in International Relations', *International Organization*, 69:2, 275–309.

48 Phillip Gary Schrank (2017) 'The Rise of Populism and the Future of NATO', *Global Politics Review*, 3:2, 53–62.

49 A key liberal internationalist is Anne-Marie Slaughter (2004) *A New World Order*. Princeton: Princeton University Press.

50 The influence of nuclear deterrence is discussed by Robert Powell (2003) 'Nuclear Deterrence Theory, Nuclear Proliferation, and National Missile Defence', *International Security*, 27:4, 86–91.

51 David Lipsey (2016) 'Liberal Interventionism', *The Political Quarterly*, 87:3, 415–23.

52 Stephen Van Evera (1998) 'Offense, Defense, and the Causes of War', *International Security*, 22:4, 5–43.

Chapter 4

Are liberal values wealthy values?

> Liberalism often claims neutrality about the choices people make in liberal society; it is the defender of 'Right', not any particular conception of the 'Good'. Yet it is not neutral about the basis on which people make their decisions ... Not only are all political and economic relationships seen as fungible and subject to constant redefinition, so are *all* relationships – to place, to neighborhood, to nation, to family, and to religion. Liberalism encourages loose connections. (Patrick J. Deneen, *Why Liberalism Failed*)[1]

Liberalism emphasizes individual rights to freedom and autonomy.[2] In Britain, the worldview was articulated by the Remain campaign, liberals recently stressing openness to external influences. Equivalents exist in other countries; among the most notable is the *La République En Marche* movement of French President Emmanuel Macron. Liberal ideas are influential across mainstream politics. Not only are the rights of minorities enshrined in law, but our political systems protect individual expression. Liberalism presents definitional challenges. An alternative meaning of liberalism, economic libertarianism, involves advocacy of free markets. I deal with this belief, associated with conservatism, in Chapter 2. I am here concerned with social liberalism.[3] This form emphasizes postmaterial values, involving freedom and autonomy, foreseeing a positive role for the state. This contrasts with economic libertarian opposition to the state, recalling objections of classic liberals who regarded state intervention as inimical to freedom.[4]

Liberals tend to be wealthier. Not only is this true historically, Marxists underlining the bourgeois character of classic liberalism,[5] but this distinguishes social liberals (see Table 4.1). In the Brexit referendum, the Remain vote was affluent; 57 per cent of voters in the AB social grade preferred to remain in the EU, falling to 40 per cent among the DE grade (see Table 3.1). In contrast to conservatives, liberals tend to be socio-cultural workers employed in interpersonal contexts, such as doctors and teachers;[6] working in such settings is associated with more egalitarian views. Education also predicts support for liberalism, apparent in Brexit voting patterns, though is related to income.[7]

The relationship between liberal views and income and education provokes vivid debate. After the Brexit vote, stunned Remainers mocked Leavers for their uneducated profile; the arguments used by the Leave campaign were equated with ignorance. I expressed this view in the shock of the morning of 24 June 2016, yet on reflection it is unsatisfactory. Though

Table 4.1   Voting in the French 2017 presidential election first round by income

	Jean-Luc Mélenchon (new left)	Emmanuel Macron (liberal)	François Fillon (conservative)	Marine Le Pen (national populist)
Total	19.2%	23.7%	19.7%	21.9%
Monthly household income				
Less than €1,250	25%	14%	12%	32%
From €1,250 to €2,000	23%	18%	15%	29%
From €2,000 to €3,000	18%	25%	17%	20%
More than €3,000	16%	32%	25%	15%

Source: Ipsos (2017).

education makes people more liberal, as discussed in Chapter 3, there is a compelling link between liberal ideas and the interests of richer citizens. Liberal values have thus evolved in a way which privileges the wealthier. Not only has this occurred historically, battles for classic liberal rights reflecting this logic, but social liberal preoccupations with professional equality and immigration reveal that it continues today. Liberalism shows the conditional relationship between ethics and interests, a phenomenon which is relevant to all worldviews.

Liberalism and wealth: a long-standing relationship

Liberalism has long been associated with the interests of the wealthy. As liberal democracy was established around him, Marx asserted that such systems were related to bourgeois self-interest.[8] Liberal rights were considered synonymous with the defence of inequality. Parliamentary power allowed for laws defending property to be established, while civil rights guaranteed the articulation of middle-class interests. One does not have to be a Marxist to appreciate such arguments. Because of their greater education and leisure time, richer classes are better placed to engage in politics. Poorer citizens, toiling under the yokes of want and precarity, are preoccupied with more mundane matters.

At a more profound level, the relationship between liberalism and wealth has exerted a long-term influence on morality itself. This is related to the intimate association between capitalism and liberalism. In the past few centuries, the former has achieved prevalence, first in the West and then globally. This has involved the dominance of values synonymous with capitalism; sociologists note the tendency of modern societies to be more individualistic, as opposed to feudal predecessors.[9] Associated with these developments is the fetishization of individual wealth. In contrast to civilizations organized on alternative lines, capitalist societies are remarkably tolerant of wealth inequalities. The following example is instructive. According to researchers, it costs a few thousand pounds to save a life in the developing world.[10] Despite this, citizens of the developed world routinely spend this sum on trifles such as holidays; this is done by people across the political spectrum and is considered normal. As I write, the realization that expenditure on my wedding could have saved lives upsets me. The argument can be localized. Why should I spend thousands on a wedding, when small children a few streets away suffer malnourishment?

The fact that this is acceptable can be traced back to our capitalist system; because we live in societies which are predicated on the generation of wealth, with accompanying inequalities within the population, ethical views which frown on such behaviour fail to take root. We are not indifferent to poverty in the West, campaigns to end local and international poverty enjoying successes, yet opposition to inequality is far from a primary value. There is admitted variance among liberals. The Liberal Democrats are notable for a social-democratic wing, distinguishing them from continental liberal parties who advocate economic libertarianism and social liberalism.[11] Despite this difference, liberals tend not to prioritize the reduction of economic inequality; Liberal Democrat complicity in austerity is instructive.

If we are to appreciate the means by which such standards emerge, it is vital to understand the diverse values which characterize human societies. As anthropologists have long recognized, different societies are characterized by distinct standards.[12] Aside from cultural curiosities, there are differences in socio-economic values. In certain tribal and communist societies, there are taboos against individual retention of significant wealth. Though research on modern attitudes shows that views within countries do not necessarily reflect levels of inequality, one study finding that attitudes in the United States and Soviet Union in 1990 were similar,[13] insights from anthropology are more significant. In certain hunter-gatherer societies, norms against individual accumulation meant that equality was socially enforced.[14] Given this diversity of values, scholars conclude that ethical principles are far from self-evident; they reflect historical contingency and societal need.

The former is difficult to pinpoint, historical influences coming from diverse sources, yet the latter is more tangible. For many years, sociologists have underlined the way in which capitalist societies engender ethics which complement the productive model. There are precedents in the work of Marx and Durkheim, yet most relevant is the contribution of Karl Mannheim: a German sociologist active during interwar years and associated with the sociology of knowledge. In *Ideology and Utopia*, Mannheim argued that ideas were 'products of their time and of the social statuses of their proponents'.[15] This has implications for the relationship between liberal economic interests and ethics. From a historical perspective, we may note how liberal attention has focused on the expansion of freedom; achievements include the abolition of slavery, widening of the suffrage and protection of the rights of minorities. Though this record is inspirational – the world would be unrecognizable without these landmarks – none of these accomplishments directly concern economic equality; rather they allow more equal participation in political and economic life. The fact that formal slavery became impermissible long ago, yet poverty which practically enslaves exists to this day, should not escape our attention.[16]

These processes have occurred by indirect means. Parallels with biological evolution are instructive. In the natural world, organisms evolve in line with structural characteristics of environments, certain mutations fitting surroundings. Though such processes are limited by existing capacity, the oddly circuitous connection between a giraffe's voice box and brain reflecting an ancestor with no neck, there is broad correspondence between evolution and need; the giraffe neck evolved to facilitate sexual competition and feeding.[17] Ideas evolve in a similar way. In any society, multiple ideas exist; a walk down any high street shows this. Not all these ideas prosper; many of the political and religious causes presented to shoppers will be just as obscure in twenty years. The emergence and success of ideas reflects existing structures, as I emphasize below, yet there is a key link with social need. Notwithstanding the genius of a thinker such as Adam Smith, discussed in Chapter 2, the popularity of Smith was related to the interests of emerging industrial classes; free markets enriched these citizens. This is like biological evolution. Diverse traits emerge in organisms, yet only those which suit environments tend to endure.

Such developments are admittedly contingent. Just as biological evolution is imperfect, as the giraffe shows, ideas evolve in an uneven way; this reflects factors such as the legacies of historic struggles or the brilliance of individual thinkers. These influences entail specific paths of development, evidenced by distinct national liberal traditions and reflecting the lock-in effects emphasized by historical institutionalists.[18] We see this in the separate routes of British and French liberalism, embarked upon centuries ago and involving different attitudes to the state.

Traditions reflect multiple preoccupations. In the case of British liberalism, there has been concern for economic inequality.[19] Anti-slavery liberals lobbied for factory acts; such legislation introduced restrictions on dangerous employment, albeit limited ones. This became part of the liberal tradition, allowing for alliances with socialists as liberalism developed. This concern endures. Research suggests that British and American liberals tend to favour redistributive politics, even when they are wealthier.[20] Despite this tendency, improvement of economic conditions has been a secondary priority, reflecting lower consistency with economic needs and failing to become pivotal. In Chapter 5, I show how priorities shape outcomes. Liberal ethics have thus been set in a capitalist cast. Rather than challenging wealth inequalities, liberalism has focused on improving equality of opportunity.

Such processes have occurred over many centuries, far beyond our control and shaping our very mindsets; given that certain liberal values seem so obvious to us, it is difficult to understand that they are not natural law. The volume of work which shows that liberal values are constructed, comprising studies of tribal societies and the development of capitalism, is nonetheless considerable.[21] Concealed though they are, such trends continue to distinguish modern liberalism. In recent decades, social liberals have responded to globalization in a way consistent with traditional values; openness has been embraced and new forms of discrimination have been combated. Consistent with historic tendencies, opposition to economic inequality has failed to mature. In addition, certain causes pursued by liberals, as we see below, have arguably undermined the position of lower classes.

How globalization has worsened tensions within liberalism

The way in which liberalism evolves to favour the richer is illustrated by the internal and external dimensions of its response to globalization. In terms of the former, social liberals have created new domestic constituencies, comprising demographics such as women, ethnic minorities and LGBT+. Echoing historic struggles for groups such as nonconformists, liberals have fought to end discrimination. Achievements are undeniable;

our societies have become more tolerant in recent decades. Despite accomplishments, these advances tend to benefit the wealthier. This is because such demands focus on the professional sphere, consistent with the interests of liberals yet less relevant to the interests of low-income citizens. This argument pertains to several groups, though the case of gender equality has attracted particular attention.

Social liberal programmes for female equality emphasize professional concerns. In recent times, issues such as pay discrimination and harassment have featured strongly in the agendas of feminists. There is a coincidence between these demands and the interests of richer, better educated women; because of their focus on professional affairs, they allow such women to maximize labour market returns. There is much work on the relationship between feminism and capitalism. In a definitive essay, Nancy Fraser argues that the utopian desires of feminists of the 1960s later legitimated globalized capitalism; because feminism embraced cultural politics, as opposed to redistribution, it became co-opted by business elites committed to individualism. Recent studies emphasize links between feminism and business in post-financial crisis efforts to achieve gender equality.[22]

Aside from radical accounts, more conservative scholars call attention to diverse female demands. As the sociologist Catherine Hakim asserts, home and family are the core preoccupation of a significant minority of women, often ignored by policymakers.[23]

Statistics affirm this; a large-scale survey by the Department of Education discovered that 54 per cent of working mothers wished to work fewer hours and spend more time looking after their children.[24] Class is associated with such attitudes, surveys showing that feminism is less popular among lower classes.[25]

These preferences are related to labour market positioning. Because low-income women are unable to take advantage of professional equality to the same extent, many desire benefits associated with the rearing of families. This is related to the poorer job prospects of such women, childcare being more appealing in such circumstances, yet it is difficult to attribute differences entirely to this. Not only will there always be poorer quality jobs, but such preferences reflect national populism; as I emphasize in Chapter 3, preservation of tradition can benefit lower classes. Overlaps between the interests of women of different incomes should not be denied, few regretting backlashes against predatory men, yet the rights favoured by women of distinct classes are discrete; some even lie in tension. In such circumstances and by the causal means which I have outlined, liberalism prioritizes its richer supporters.

In terms of its external response to globalization, social liberalism has embraced immigration, advocating freedom of movement. This is related to heightened levels of immigration, occurring across the world because of greater mobility associated with globalization. In the British case, immigration is related to EU membership, the 2004 decision to open borders to

Central and Eastern European (CEE) member states encouraging migration from these countries.

Though there are general benefits of immigration, including cultural diversity and strengthening of fiscal capacity, advantages are skewed towards the richer. Not only does immigration lower prices in certain sectors used by the better-off,[26] but the wealthier face fewer unsettling effects. These individuals work in occupations which are not subject to significant competition from immigrants and, because of better education, are more relaxed about contact with different cultures. Underpinning these factors are the looser bonds which tie such groups to specific localities.[27] Even if these citizens live in particular places, their superior mobility means that they have less stake in the endurance of communities. The capacity of richer groups to benefit from emigration should also be emphasized. As a result of their superior position on the labour market, the wealthy have more to gain from the opening of foreign borders. Given disadvantages of emigration for poorer citizens in sender countries,[28] assessed in Chapter 3, tendencies for international organizations to promote freedom of movement can be interpreted as transnational alliances of middle classes; there are benefits for the wealthy in destination and sender countries. European freedom of movement works on this basis; it is most keenly advocated by parties with richer support bases.

The causes reviewed above have become prominent because they are consistent with liberal economic interests. As I have emphasized, the emergence of specific ethical positions is far from inevitable; there are multiple directions in which ethics might evolve. In the case of twenty-first century social liberalism, values have developed which are consistent with the interests of mobile, wealthy citizens. Rather than stigmatizing those who spend considerable sums on non-imperative goods or disrupt conditions in local communities, coincidence with self-interest has meant that liberal values have coalesced around particular issues.

Changes in transmission mechanisms are noteworthy. When Mannheim theorized the means by which ideas spread, classic means of diffusion prevailed. These included newspapers, public meetings and local political parties; in ensuing decades, radio and television would become important. Though such mechanisms remain crucial, recent changes have been transformative. Social media is key.[29] The influence of institutions such as Facebook and Twitter can be overstated, particular classes always grouping together, yet there are vital implications for articulation between class and ideas. Social media has quickened political socialization. Not only did traditional institutions such as newspapers and party meetings exert a filter influence, sifting eccentric views, but they used pre-internet forms of technology, slowing circulation speeds. Social media is different; based on instantaneous exchange of information, it facilitates direct exchange between citizens in a way which traditional institutions did not, creating echo chambers and facilitating contact with

international counterparts. Circumvention of traditional barriers allows ideas consistent with interests to
emerge more swiftly. This does not necessarily favour
any worldview, yet liberal ideas have fared well; social
media is associated with rising support for causes such
as gender equality and LGBT+ rights.[30]

Liberal successes are associated with another feature of social media; the medium increases incentives
for displays of affiliation.[31] Human need for approval
is deep-rooted. Once specific ideas achieve dominance
within communities, there is motivation for members
to pronounce them; this has long been evident in religious groups. Liberalism is vulnerable to this. Because
of the ethical form assumed by liberal views, conservative ideas expressing resistance to change, there is
incentive for their display. Such processes have taken
place for years – in academia and the public sector
espousal of liberal views has long allowed the speaker
to assure colleagues that (s)he is one of them – yet
social media has increased this effect. The medium allows uniform statements to be shared instantly with
thousands of like-minded colleagues; this is rich soil
for the diffusion of liberal views. Long-term effects of
social media remain unknown. Despite this caveat,
the significance of the medium must be recognized;
it recasts the terms in which class and ideas interact
and contemporary liberalism reflects its logic. Whether
the influence of social media is desirable is a different
question; critics associate it with partisanship and aggression.[32] I reflect on this in Chapter 6.

Wealth is admittedly an imperfect predictor of tolerance. As is well known, the rich can be prejudiced; several national-populist parties have moneyed leaders. Some social liberal causes also have a looser association with class. LGBT+ rights are pursued with traditional emphasis on individual liberty, which is related to class, yet the relationship with economic interests is less direct; this demonstrates the force of ideas, in this case the liberal dedication to justice for all. Because of liberal commitment to certain causes, ideas obtain autonomy, sometimes allowing them to overcome structural constraints; studies of the role of ideas in promoting same-sex union laws show this.[33] Despite these caveats, it is difficult to deny the relationship between liberalism, affluence and certain issues. This is demonstrated by studies which show that wealth predicts support for liberal causes. A recent survey of professional and unskilled workers asked whether immigration had enriched culture and benefited the economy; it found that assent among professionals was around 30 percentage points higher.[34] There are similar data on issues such as the death penalty.[35] Beyond specific topics, liberal support bases have been wealthy across epochs and countries. It is difficult to believe that such movements could *not* produce positions which advantage supporters.

Social liberal commitment to individual rights is inseparable from international advocacy of liberal politics. Institutions such as the EU and NATO have endorsed liberalism, supported by domestic liberal constituencies. This promotes global stability; national democracy allows expression of diverse interests, while liberal multilateralism promotes peaceful compromise. International relations scholars emphasize the importance of such relationships, noting the role of America as an underwriter.[36] Despite this record, there has been recent tension between national and international liberalism. Globalization has weakened the relationship between liberalism and national democracy, a process quickened by the success of national populism. This is a liberal form of externalization; it upsets the traditional balance between domestic and international liberal democracy, making reconciliation of diverse interests more difficult.

Though the relationship between liberalism and the democratic nation state is historically umbilical, liberals organizing at this level from the nineteenth century, factors such as the opening of borders and cheaper travel have weakened this association. In a globalized world, liberal horizons are increasingly post-national. This reflects the superior relocation capacity of the wealthy. Economic implications have attracted most attention, scholars emphasizing the ability of footloose firms to extract concessions from workforces and governments,[37] yet political consequences are crucial. Because of their enhanced exit power, liberals have less cause for commitment to specific polities. This has been evident in the Brexit debate. I have heard numerous wealthy citizens threaten to leave the country should Brexit go badly;

I have heard few poor citizens say this. Not all liberals show such weakening commitment, many being dedicated to specific communities, yet prevalence among certain liberals implies change in the character of the worldview.

Reflecting this disconnection, many social liberals identify with international organizations such as the EU and UN, regarding these institutions as pivotal sources of rights; documents such as the EU Charter of Fundamental Rights and Universal Declaration of Human Rights are revered. These texts embody liberal principles, yet their democratic mandate is less obvious. Scholars have long recognized democratic deficits associated with supranational institutions.[38] Though the EU obtains democratic legitimacy from its parliament, citizens remain attached to national institutions and show little interest in transnational bodies; few Europeans can name their MEPs. Despite such problems, certain liberals consider supranational rights to be particularly legitimate. A colleague of mine, the Brexit-supporting economist Kent Matthews, relates a conversation with his daughter Selena prior to the referendum. Expressing preference for Remain, Selena asserted that rights were now more important than democracy.

These developments are concerning. Liberal disembeddedness implies weakening of the links between domestic and international liberalism, with consequences for global stability. Recently, such trends have worsened; as national-populist and new-left parties have prospered, liberal dedication to national democracy has shown signs of ebbing. In recent years, liberals have written high-profile books which dismiss democracy, titles including *Against Democracy* and *Against Elections*.[39] These sentiments are far from universal – British liberals tend to evaluate democracy more positively than conservatives and national populists[40] – yet appetite for such arguments is worrying. Politically, one thinks of the People's Vote campaign. Exaggerating misconduct of Leave and ignoring multimillion-pound governmental support for Remain, this movement overlooked the results of a major democratic exercise. It pains me to write this; I was one of the keenest Remain activists in Wales during the 2016 campaign.

This is a form of externalization. Though less dangerous than the national-populist externalization assessed in Chapter 3, the weakening relationship between liberalism and national democracy threatens stability. Liberal-democratic structures are best placed to resolve conflicts of interest. Not only does universal suffrage allow citizens to articulate preferences, but deliberative institutions permit consideration of different viewpoints, promoting balanced outcomes. This does not always occur in practice, as critics emphasize, yet alternative models are less effective.[41] Aside from well-known problems with dictatorships, the rights-based supranational systems advocated by certain liberals have problems responding to voter concerns; crises of confidence in the EU show this. If liberal self-interest is to be reconciled with wider needs, it is vital that liberalism reconnects with national democracy; this was a traditional strength and underpinned achievements of liberal internationalism. There are now structural pressures in opposite directions, meaning that challenges will be difficult to address, yet global stability depends upon resolution. In the appendix, I consider how liberal thinkers might approach this problem.

Given the depth of liberal principles, some will be sensitive to points I have made in this chapter. In conclusion, I must state that I do not mean to oppose liberal values. The achievements of liberalism are formidable; liberal opposition to discrimination has unlocked human potential and made our societies kinder. Liberal alliances in the international sphere have guaranteed democracy; as the case of national populism shows, such institutions are vital. I am also not a relativist. Karl Mannheim, who demonstrated the relationship between ideology and interest, rejected relativism,[42] asserting that certain truths were transcendent.

I have merely attempted to show that social liberalism is not self-evidently correct and is associated with the interests of certain citizens. This is a point worth making; too many liberals, particularly in Brexit Britain, consider opponents to be stupid and/ or immoral. If such misunderstandings could be overcome, based on recognition of limits of the liberal worldview, our political culture would be healthier.

Notes

1 Patrick J. Deneen (2018) *Why Liberalism Failed*. Connecticut: Yale University Press, 34.

2 Michael Freeden and Marc Stears (2013) 'Liberalism', in M. Freeden, L. T. Sargent and M. Stears (eds), *The Oxford Handbook of Political Ideologies*. Oxford: Oxford University Press, 329–47.

3 In Britain, supporters of social liberalism often oppose economic libertarianism; these are known as left-liberals. The Liberal Democrats are broadly left-liberal, though include some economic libertarians.

4 Postmaterial politics is elaborated by Ronald Inglehart (1977) *The Silent Revolution: Changing Values and Political Styles among Western Publics*. Princeton: Princeton University Press. Different forms of liberalism are identified by Andrew Vincent (1998) 'New Ideologies for Old?', *The Political Quarterly*, 69:1, 49–51.

5 Richard Ashcraft (1972) 'Marx and Weber on Liberalism as Bourgeois Ideology', *Comparative Studies in Society and History*, 14:2, 130–68.

6 Herbert Kitschelt (1994) *The Transformation of European Social Democracy*. Cambridge: Cambridge University Press, 16–17; Daniel Oesch (2008) 'The Changing Shape of Class Voting: An Individual-Level Analysis of Party Support in Britain, Germany and Switzerland', *European Societies*, 10:3, 329–55.

7 Sara B. Hobolt (2016) 'The Brexit Vote: A Divided Nation, a Divided Continent', *Journal of European Public Policy*, 23:9, 1259–77.

8 Scholars disagree on whether Marx critiqued specific rights of capitalist society, rather than universal rights. Moorby's critique of Lukes is informative, Steven Lukes (1982) 'Can a Marxist Believe in Human Rights?', *Praxis International*, 1:4, 334–45; Martin Moorby (2018) 'Who is this Man Who is Distinct from this Citizen: Revisiting Marx's Critique of Liberal Rights', *Journal of Cultural Studies of Association*, 7:1.

9 Nuances of this relationship are discussed by Bryan S. Turner (1998) 'Individualism, Capitalism and the Dominant Culture: A Note on the Debate', *The Australian and New Zealand Journal of Sociology*, 24:1, 47–64.

10 Christopher Murray and Ray Chambers (2015) 'Keeping Score: Fostering Accountability for Children's Lives', *The Lancet*, 386:98, 5–10.

11 Examples include La République En Marche! (France), Freie Demokratische Partei (FDP; Germany) and Ciudadanos (Spain).

12 This field is introduced by Matthew Engelke (2019) *How to Think Like an Anthropologist*. Princeton: Princeton University Press.

13 Robert J. Shiller, Maxim Boycko and Vladimir Korobov (1990) 'Popular Attitudes towards Free Markets: The Soviet Union and the United States Compared', *American Economic Review*, 8:3, 385–400. Broader international attitudes are discussed by Lars Osberg and Timothy Smeeding (2004) 'Fair Inequality? An International Comparison of Attitudes to Pay Differentials', Dalhousie University. Available at: www. wwwcpr.maxwell.syr.edu/faculty/smeeding/selectedpapers/ Economicaversion27October2004.pdf. Accessed 17 May 2020.

14 James Woodburn (1982) 'Egalitarian Societies', *Man New Series*, 17:3, 431–51.

15 Karl Mannheim (1960) *Ideology and Utopia: An Introduction to the Sociology of Knowledge*. London: Routledge.

16 This is an old Marxist argument. 'The slave is sold once and for all; the proletarian must sell himself daily and hourly. The individual slave, property of one master, is assured an existence, however miserable it may be, because of the master's interest. The individual proletarian, property as it were of the entire bourgeois class which buys his labor only when someone has need of it, has no secure existence. This existence is assured only to the class as a whole.' Friedrich Engels (1969) *The Principles of Communism*. Moscow: Progress Publishers.

17 Australian Academy of Science (2018) 'Why Evolution Isn't Perfect'. Available at: www.science.org.au/curious/ earth-environment/why-evolution-isnt-perfect. Accessed 19

January 2020. There is disagreement on the origins of the giraffe neck. Some argue that it helps feeding, while others emphasize its use in male duels. See Rob E. Simmons and Res Altwegg (2010) 'Necks-for-Sex or Competing Browsers? A Critique of Ideas on the Evolution of Giraffe', *Journal of Zoology*, 282:1, 6–12.

18 Kathleen Thelen (1999) 'Historical Institutionalism in Comparative Politics', *Annual Review of Political Science*, 2:1, 369–404.

19 Alan Sykes (1997) *The Rise and Fall of British Liberalism: 1776–1988*. London: Routledge.

20 Jonathan Mellon and Christopher Prosser (2017) 'Authoritarianism, Social Structure and Economic Policy Preferences', Social Science Research Network.

21 E.g. Ulrich Beck (2012) 'Individualism', in G. Ritzer (ed.), *The Wiley-Blackwell Encyclopaedia of Globalization*. New Jersey: Blackwell; Louis Dumont (1992) *Essays on Individualism: Modern Ideology in Anthropological Perspective*. Chicago: University of Chicago Press; Larry Siedentop (2014) *Inventing the Individual*. Cambridge, MA: Harvard University Press; Woodburn, 'Egalitarian Societies'.

22 Nancy Fraser (2013) 'Feminism, Capitalism, and the Cunning of History', in *Fortunes of Feminism: From State-Managed Capitalism to Neoliberal Crisis*. London: Verso, 209–27; Adrienne Roberts (2012) 'Financial Crisis, Financial Firms … and Financial Feminism? The Rise of "Transnational Business Feminism" and the Necessity of Marxist-Feminist IPE', *Socialist Studies*, 8:2, 85–108.

23 Catherine Hakim (2000) *Work-Lifestyle Choices in the 21st Century: Preference Theory*. Oxford: Oxford University Press.

24 Tom Huskinson, Sylvie Hobden, Dominic Oliver, Jennifer Keyes, Mandy Littlewood, Julia Pye and Sarah Tipping (2016) 'Childcare and Early Years Survey of Parents 2014–2015', The UK Government Publication – Department for Education. Available at: www.gov.uk/government/statistics/childcare-and-early-years-survey-of-parents-2014-to-2015. Accessed 17 May 2020.

25 Eleanor Attar Taylor and Jacqueline Scott (2018) 'Gender: New Consensus or Continuing Battleground?', in D. Phillips, J. Curtice, M. Phillips and J. Perry (eds), *British Social Attitudes: The 35th Report*. London: The National Centre for Social Research, 8; YouGov (2018) 'Survey Results'. Available at: www.d25d2506sfb94s.cloudfront.net/cumulus_uploads/document/iopahgu564/InternalResults_180205_Feminism_Suffragettes_w.pdf. Accessed 1 February 2020.

26 Tommaso Frattini (2014) 'Impact of Migration on UK Consumer Prices'. Available at: https://assets.publishing.service.gov.uk/government/uploads/system/uploads/attachment_data/file/328006/Impact_of_migration_on_UK_consumer_prices__2014.pdf. Accessed 17 May 2020, 26–7.

27 Hanspeter Kriesi, Edgar Grande, Romain Lachat, Martin Dolezal, Simon Bornschier and Timotheos Frey (2008) *West European Politics in the Age of Globalization*. Cambridge: Cambridge University Press, 5.

28 Atis Berzins and Peteris Zvidrins (2011) 'Depopulation in the Baltic States', *Lithuanian Journal of Statistics*, 50:1, 39–48.

29 Daniel Trottier and Christian Fuchs (2014) *Social Media, Politics and the State: Protests, Revolutions, Riots, Crime and Policing in the Age of Facebook, Twitter and YouTube*. London: Routledge.

30 Amy B. Becker and Lauren Copeland (2016) 'Networked Publics: How Connective Social Media Use Facilitates Political Consumerism Among LGBT Americans', *Journal of Information Technology & Politics*, 13:1, 22–36.

31 Elaine Wallace, Isabel Buil and Leslie De Chernatony (2018) '"Consuming Good" on Social Media: What Can Conspicuous Virtue Signalling on Facebook Tell Us About Prosocial and Unethical Intentions?', *Journal of Business Ethics*, 162:1, 557–92.

32 Ariel Hasell and Brian E. Weeks (2016) 'Partisan Provocation: The Role of Partisan News Use and Emotional Responses in Political Information Sharing in Social Media', *Human Communication Research*, 42:4, 641–61.

33 Kelly Kollman (2014) 'Deploying Europe: The Creation of Discursive Imperatives for Same-Sex Unions', in D.

Paternotte and P. Ayoub (eds), *LGBT Activism and the Making of Europe*. London: Palgrave Macmillan, 97–118.

34 Robert Ford and Kitty Lymperopoulou (2017) 'Immigration'. *British Social Attitudes 34*. Available at: www.bsa.natcen. ac.uk/media/39148/bsa34_immigration_final.pdf. Accessed 17 May 2020.

35 Geoffrey Evans and James Tilley (2017) *The New Politics of Class: The Political Exclusion of the British Working Class*. Oxford: Oxford University Press, 72–5.

36 John J. Mearsheimer (2010) 'Why is Europe Peaceful Today?', *European Political Science*, 9:3, 387–97.

37 Wolfgang Streeck (1998) 'The Internationalization of Industrial Relations in Europe: Prospects and Problems', *Politics & Society*, 26:4, 429–59.

38 'Undemocratic liberalism' is discussed by Yascha Mounk (2018) *The People vs. Democracy: Why Our Freedom is in Danger and How to Save It*. Cambridge, MA: Harvard University Press. The EU democratic deficit is evaluated by Andreas Follesdal and Simon Hix (2006) 'Why there is a Democratic Deficit in the EU: A Response to Majone and Moravcsik', *Journal of Common Market Studies*, 44:3, 533–62.

39 E.g. Jason Brennan (2016) *Against Democracy*. Princeton: Princeton University Press; David Harsanyi (2014) *The People Have Spoken (and They Are Wrong): The Case Against Democracy*. Washington, DC: Regnery; David Van Reybrouck (2016) *Against Elections: The Case for Democracy*. London: Bodley Head.

40 See my analysis of British Election Study (BES) data, Thomas Prosser (2020) 'Who are the New Conservative Voters and What Socio-Economic Policies Do They Want? Some Pre-Budget Analysis', blog entry. Available at: https:// thomasjprosser.wordpress.com/2020/03/10/who-are-the-new-conservative-voters-and-what-socio-economic-policies-do-they-want-some-pre-budget-analysis/. Accessed 17 May 2020.

41 Deliberative democracy is elaborated by Joshua Cohen (1997) 'Deliberation and Democratic Legitimacy', in J. Bohman and W. Rehg (eds), *Deliberative Democracy: Essays on Reason*

and Politics. Cambridge, MA: Massachusetts Institute of Technology Press, 67–92. For the argument that capitalism undermines democracy, see Wolfgang Streeck (2016) *How Will Capitalism End? Essays on a Failing System*. New York: Verso Books.

42 Markus Seidel (2011) 'Relativism or Relationism? A Mannheimian Interpretation of Fleck's Claims about Relativism', *Journal for General Philosophy of Science*, 42:2, 219–40.

Chapter 5

The new left: all about that base

Alberto Garzón: 'There's still a lot of work to do among abstainers, like the marginalized people in my home region of Malaga who won't have a sandwich to eat this Christmas.'
Jean-Luc Mélenchon: 'Don't fool yourself Alberto, the poor aren't going to vote. You must learn from the Latin American experience. You win with the support of the middle classes; once you're in office, you can reach the marginalized with social policy.' (Meeting between French new-left leader Jean-Luc Mélenchon and Spanish left-wing leaders, Madrid, January 2015)[1]

The rise of the new left[2] reflects crises of the twenty-first century. In recent years, as a result of falling levels of growth, pressure has been put on the position of the middle classes. Younger members of this group, often locked out of housing and labour markets, have been particularly hit. In these circumstances, the young middle classes have been radicalized. Though adopting traditional radical language, the writings of Karl Marx being popular, new-left movements differ from older equivalents. Traditional left-wing parties, from social democrats to communists, were primarily supported by lower classes. The new left is different.[3] Not only was the support base of the Corbyn Labour Party in 2017 and 2019 elections comparatively wealthy (see Figure 5.1), but analysis suggests that radical left activists are relatively affluent.[4] Trends are similar in other countries. In the Spanish 2015 election, the new-left Podemos party was more popular among richer groups.[5] In the United States, Bernie Sanders suffered from a similar problem, even if the American context is distinct.[6]

Though supporters of Jeremy Corbyn have organized through the Labour Party, the traditional party of the working class, this is a curiosity associated with British politics; the First Past the Post (FPTP) system discriminates against smaller parties which are not geographically concentrated. In other European countries, the formation of new parties, such as Podemos and La France Insoumise, shows the distinctiveness of the new left. On the one hand, new-left parties adopt highly liberal positions on social issues; radical feminists and LGBT+ activists find homes in these movements. Certain tensions inherent in liberalism, discussed in Chapter 4, therefore exist in the new left. On the other hand, emphasis is placed on the redistribution of resources. This is related to the roots of the new left, many older members long being involved in Marxist politics, yet also reflects the wishes of a new generation; younger members desire a more equal economy.[7]

All about that base

In this chapter, I argue that new-left parties inadvertently favour the younger, wealthier followers of such movements. Even if these parties espouse economic justice, their programmes are likely to shift resources from the rich to the young middle classes, leaving the poorest in a similar position. This reflects a tendency for parties to favour their support bases, rooted in the human inclination to prioritize personal need. Though the new left is now in retreat, losing the 2019 General Election and Labour leadership, it remains a crucial force. The Starmer Labour Party also has wealthier supporters,[8] even if more careful language lessens tension between rhetoric and support base. Given these considerations, the case of the new left remains essential.

Despite tendencies to compensate supporters, new-left parties are not mere vehicles for the self-interest of followers. Political movements are also depositories of tradition, reflecting the influence of historical struggles. This combines with the contemporary values of supporters, some of which are non-material, resulting in worldviews which are indirectly related to self-interest. This is evident in new-left foreign policy. For over a century, Marxists have resisted imperialism, resulting in links with various anti-imperial causes; opposition to Israeli foreign policy is the best known.[9] This conflict may have little direct connection with the deteriorating economic position of young Westerners, yet it is partly for historical reasons that such causes stir followers of the new left; opposition to colonialism is central to radical identity. Isolationism associated with anti-imperialism arguably encourages conflict, as with national-populist isolationism, yet links with new-left ideas are less obvious. In Chapter 6, I discuss the capacity of the new left and social democracy to resolve externalization.

Anti-imperial causes are also associated with opposition to capitalism, undoubtedly relevant to the economic interests of new-left supporters. Marxists stress the interconnectedness of struggles, asserting that a precondition to justice is the overthrow of the global system. According to this view, revolution will end systemic injustices of capitalism, inaugurating societies which fulfil the interests of all.[10] The feasibility of revolution is another question. Given the fate of previous experiments with communism, all of which failed to attain initial goals, many will understand my scepticism. Such disappointments were the result of numerous factors, yet it is worth underlining the problem of institutional rupture. As emphasized in Chapter 2, humans behave unpredictably in times of systemic breakdown, making revolutions hazardous. Problems with existing systems can also be insuperable, as previous revolutionaries have discovered. A modern revolution is moreover a distant prospect; even followers of the new left consider it unrealistic.[11]

Because revolution is unfeasible, the new left is cursed to work within the imperfect existing world. This is characterized by a basic problem: scarcity. As

Marxists themselves assert,[12] capitalist societies have finite resources, which must be divided between competing interests. All parties are poor at conveying the problem of scarcity to voters; bad news is electorally unpopular and politicians, by fair means or foul, prefer to avoid divulging it. New-left parties are particularly bad at this. Though such movements tend not to call for the overthrow of capitalism, a system in which Marxists regard scarcity as endemic, such parties emphasize the potential of their programmes to bring about justice. This is based on expansionary economic policies, often ambitious yet falling short of a break with capitalism, and residual commitment to the overthrow of institutions; new-left policymakers believe that their programmes will hasten transition to a post-capitalist world.

In conditions in which radical parties are reluctant to concede scarcity, but the phenomenon persists anyway, a fascinating effect takes place; the supporters of such movements compensate themselves ahead of others. Such an outcome may not be premeditated, yet occurs in circumstances in which abundance does not materialize and humans retain a subliminal capacity to safeguard their own interests. This took place in communist states. In societies in which rank scarcity was overseen by party elites, apparatchiks enjoyed luxuries denied to the population. We may note that this was never planned, occurring incrementally as elites encountered abundance. New-left parties are more committed to liberal-democratic values, yet rudiments of

these processes remain in place. Humans tend to prioritize their own needs, particularly when organized in
large groups. This is obvious in the case of conservative parties, yet new-left emphasis on universal justice
makes the movement fascinating. If principles will
ever overcome self-interest, it is in this case.

If we are to understand the way in which humans
compensate themselves in policy processes, it is vital
to acquaint ourselves with relevant stages. A first
problem emerges during the articulation of concerns.
Members of the new left claim that their demands
encompass all oppressed groups. Not only do the slo-
gans of such movements aim at this, 'for the many, not
the few' being a famous example, but time is dedicated
to campaigns for international justice; new left opposition to imperialism is well known.

Despite such ambitions, limits on time and awareness mean that it is impossible to be equally attentive
to all relevant issues; certain goals are prioritized. As
I emphasize above, the international campaigns which
interest the new left follow a particular logic, reflecting long-standing preoccupations. Economic concerns are more telling. Although the new left desires
general redistribution, primary attention is paid to
issues which affect support bases. In the British case,
the wealthier profile of new-left supporters means
that concerns such as tuition fees and public services
are prioritized. These issues do not always advantage
the richer, as poorer citizens also attend university
and use public services, yet research indicates such

a relationship. The ending of tuition fees would be regressive; a study of their abolition in Scotland described free tuition as 'the perfect middle-class, feel-good policy'.[13] The greater tendency of middle classes to benefit from public services is well-established, one study speaking of 'sharp elbows' associated with cultural capital;[14] poorer citizens are more sensitive to changes in benefits.[15]

New-left supporters will reply that, in addition to issues such as tuition fees and public services, they endorse causes which help poorer citizens. This is undeniable. For many years, the new left has campaigned to end domestic and international poverty; issues such as benefit cuts, child poverty and conditions in sub-Saharan Africa have attracted attention.[16] Commitment to these causes is impressive and reminds us of the power of ideas. Research also suggests that party agendas are not mere functions of support bases. In a study of campaign statements in the early 2000s, Geering and Häusermann found that left-wing parties with wealthier bases tend to remain committed to redistribution.[17] Yet this phenomenon has since heightened and, as we will see, the record of the Corbyn Labour Party on low-income issues was unexceptional. The fact that genuine poverty touches few new-left supporters means that such problems tend to become secondary goals. Humans are most concerned with their own needs. Because of limits on experience and information, we subliminally prioritize issues which affect us directly.

A personal example is instructive. Last year, a local reporter asked me to participate in a vox pop on the state of British trains. My hackles immediately rose. Recalling the occasions on which I had spent £100 on a second-class return journey from Cardiff to London, subsequently enduring crowded and ageing carriages, I declared that the quality of trains was one of the worst things about Britain. Reflection raises several questions. Are trains really a worse problem than desultory levels of benefits? What about crises of homelessness and domestic violence? If one thinks about it, there are many issues which are more serious than trains. One asks why I believed trains to be one of the worst things about Britain. The answer is inseparable from my person; trains are the preoccupation of the mobile middle classes, people far removed from genuine poverty.

I should not be too hard on myself. My reaction that day, rooted in my own experience of the world, was entirely human and indicative of our biased minds. Political processes aggregate such experiences. Party supporters consume similar media, creating narratives which reflect predominant concerns; this is amplified by the echo chambers of social media. Party structures consolidate such pressures. Issues which most preoccupy activists are raised in constituency meetings, subsequently constraining MPs. Such influences are a key constraint on the new left; because of the difficulties which humans encounter overcoming the limits of their own experiences, it is unlikely that economic justice will be achieved with a wealthy support base.

Certain features of the new left mean that this tendency is self-reinforcing. As emphasized above, such movements also support liberal causes such as immigration and LGBT+ rights, often in a militant fashion. Given that some of these issues lie in tension with the values of low-income voters, as stressed in Chapter 3, such citizens are driven away from new-left parties. In the 2019 election, the Conservative Party performed better among lower-class voters than the Labour Party (see Figure 5.1), remarkable given the roots of the Labour Party. There is scope for solidarity between poor citizens and minorities – legal aid is an immigration issue while under-25s housing benefit is an LGBT+ problem – yet this appears difficult to realize in practice.

The absence of poorer voters compounds the difficulties of the new left. Because these citizens endure low incomes, there is a link between desired policies and narrowing of inequality. Their exit deprives the new left of such voices, accentuating the demands of wealthier groups. The strength of the new left on social media is unconducive to self-reflection. As emphasized in Chapter 4, this medium encourages partisanship and exhibitionism; these are not auspicious conditions for the supple policy thinking which would help the new left overcome constraints.

In a subsequent step, issues are framed in policy programmes. This also reflects scarcity. As with party supporters, policymakers are limited in terms of the issues which they can address, while there are specific factors which constrain them. Time in parliament is valuable and space in manifestos is short; because of these limitations, only the most pressing problems, typically reflecting the needs of supporters, tend to be prioritized. Political scientists have long recognized the importance of relationships with support groups, even if there is disagreement over the significance of core and potential supporters.[18] In the case of the new left, core and swing voters tend to be middle-income groups. During the 2019 election campaign, Labour made late appeals on WASPI women and train ticket prices, both concerns of middle-class swing voters.[19]

There are also financial constraints. New-left movements can be vague about this, a habit encouraged by lack of governing experience, yet in certain circumstances are forced to make firm commitments. The 2017 and 2019 Labour manifestos were illustrative. Though pledging to abolish tuition fees, there was little action on benefit cuts introduced by Conservative governments. Even if this was a sin of omission, it was remarkable given the effects of such cuts on the poorest. I once asked a senior Corbyn ally about the matter and, after emphasizing that he had not advocated the measure himself, he was admirably honest; because of the influx of students into the party and subsequent commitments on tuition fees, there was little money left to reverse benefit cuts.

Evidence shows the tendency of new-left policy programmes to privilege middle classes. Institute for

Fiscal Studies (IFS) analysis found that the 2017 Labour manifesto redistributed resources to middle-income deciles rather than the poorest; the Liberal Democrat manifesto was more redistributive.[20] Measures such as the removal of the public sector pay cap were ostensibly progressive, yet tended to benefit the richer citizens who are employed in the public sector.[21] Though the 2019 manifesto was judged more progressive by the IFS, the document proposing abolition of the two-child limit on welfare support, there were similar problems; 'relatively modest' working-age welfare proposals reversed just over half the cuts introduced since 2015 and less than a quarter of those since 2010.[22] Investigations of other contexts reach similar conclusions. In a study of European countries, Gingrich and Häusermann[23] show that left-wing governments with strong working-class support provide more generous unemployment benefits than those with wealthier bases.

Given that new-left parties have yet to hold office, aside from countries such as Greece in which conditions are challenging, there are few data on performance while in government; Gingrich and Häusermann's work mainly concerns social-democratic parties. When office is assumed, challenges will be significant. Governing parties, whether of left or right, are struck by unpredictable scarcity. Innumerable requests are made of government, yet only some of these can be met; even in the most abundant contexts, resources are scarce. Because of political difficulties associated with raising taxation and the possibility of external crises, such as the one which affected the world in 2008, the availability of resources is also unpredictable.

In these circumstances, redistribution follows a complex logic. On the one hand, governments try to be fair. As stressed in Chapter 2, most governments in liberal democracies pursue the common good; this is ensured by the link between citizenry and sovereignty. Given the commitment of the new left to fairness, encapsulated in the Corbynite pledge to govern for the many rather than the few, new-left governments might be particularly dedicated to this goal. On the other hand, governments tend to redistribute to best positioned groups. Because of their electoral importance, the demands of core voters receive particular attention; it is these citizens who put governments in office and are vital to re-election.[24] The capacity of governments to redistribute can be overrated, research showing that major reductions in inequality are associated with events such as war or revolution,[25] yet studies suggest a relationship between support bases and redistribution. The poorer support base of New Labour was associated with redistribution to these groups. IFS analysis shows that the poorest fifth of citizens gained over 10 per cent of net income in tax and benefit changes from 1997 to 2010, the richest deciles losing net income.[26]

Given the emphasis which new-left movements place on fairness, my argument will be controversial. New-left supporters might assert that the vigour of their ideas is sufficient. According to this position, the transformative effect of new-left principles, emphasizing fairness for all and shared by leadership and grassroots, will guarantee that priority is given to the most deserving. This is implicit in the analysis of French new-left leader Jean-Luc Mélenchon, cited at the start of this chapter. The strength of new-left principles should not be dismissed. Such ideas have changed politics, bringing welcome emphasis on economic justice. This is consistent with discursive institutionalism,[27] elaborated in earlier chapters.

Such interpretations nonetheless underestimate structural constraints, analysing groups as if they are individuals. Individuals can reflect on their priorities; a conscientious member of the new left might reason that raising benefits is a greater priority than tuition fee abolition. This is unfeasible among larger groups. Because of the large number of people involved, many of whom will not be particularly interested in politics, reflection will be confined to outliers; preferences advantageous to the group will predominate, directing agendas. For these reasons, it is difficult to credit the argument of Mélenchon. The strategy of focusing on middle classes, explicit in the French case and at least implicit in other contexts, is merely likely to encourage redistribution to richer citizens. Middle classes may be crucial to welfare coalitions,[28] supporters of universal policies long recognizing their importance, yet predomination creates problems.

Ironically, Marx emphasized the links between support bases and redistribution, regarding workers as the core of left-wing parties; material interests of workers ensured that such movements would advance redistributive goals, contrasting with the secondary importance of ideas. Even if a role was conceded to a vanguard of intellectuals, this group was comparatively tiny. Marxist-Leninists emphasized this vanguard,[29] yet scarcely foresaw a socialist party with a wealthy base. Political movements advance the interests of the groups which they represent. This principle is perennial because it is obvious. This is particularly the case with mass movements, in which the preferences of outlying individuals become subsumed.

We may wonder whether new-left elites appreciate such issues. A figure such as Mélenchon is aware that his supporters are wealthier. Recognition that this problem restricts redistributive potential is not so evident, even if my source acknowledged that this was the case with tuition fees. I suspect that some elites do ponder this issue; individuals have greater reflective capacity. Concerns will nonetheless be crowded out by the non-concern of other elites, as with the apprehensions of conscientious supporters. Even if there were perfect awareness among leaders, the demands of supporters would nonetheless be more significant. As I have argued, support base preferences drive agendas and large groups tend not to forsake their interests. This invites reflection on the use of any policy suggestion (!), an issue which I consider in conclusion.

Can the new left overcome constraints?

As the new left develops, it may attract low-income supporters. Given the emphasis placed upon redistribution, this is far from impossible; new-left ideas are potentially appealing to poorer citizens and unattractive aspects may become less prominent. The German new-left movement Aufstehen has adopted such a strategy, appealing to low-income voters through opposition to migration. Many will point to existing working-class supporters of the new left. Not only was Corbyn popular among poorer members in the 2016 Labour leadership election,[30] but Labour performed reasonably among the DE social grade in the 2017 and 2019 elections (see Figure 5.1). Though there are undoubtedly working-class new-left supporters, such statistics are misleading. The Labour leader is chosen by members, a very small portion of the population, while 2017 and 2019 Labour support bases were wealthier than previous elections.

Loss of working-class support is not unique to the new left. Social-democratic parties across the West suffer this problem.[31] In the case of the Labour Party, it started at the time of New Labour; though Blair governments were primarily supported by low-income citizens, the structure of support for Brown in 2010 was like that achieved by Corbyn in 2017. The new left is nonetheless touched acutely. The phenomenon escalated under Corbyn and cases in other countries, more illustrative as the new left form separate parties, reveal this to be a particular problem. The French case could be clearer, Mélenchon achieving respectable figures among low-income voters (see Table 4.1), yet the Spanish case is egregious; Podemos support is more concentrated among wealthy citizens than support for the Spanish conservative party.[32]

Challenges discussed in this chapter are thus broad ones. The end of the Corbyn leadership has brought

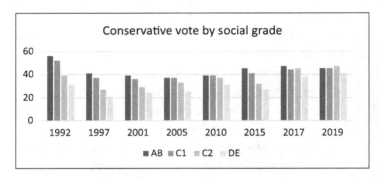

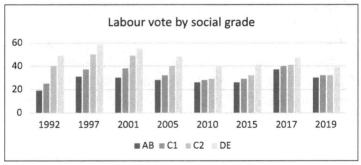

Figure 5.1 Support for British parties by social grade, 1997–2019.

no resolution. Though Keir Starmer polls better among low-income voters,[33] Labour support remains concentrated among socio-cultural professionals. In Chapter 6, I discuss challenges which social democrats face in this area.

It may be that national populists are best placed to achieve redistribution. In many countries, there are large national-populist movements with support bases which are poorer than left-wing rivals. Many advocate redistribution; PiS (Poland) and Rassemblement National (France) are prominent examples. In these cases, it is difficult to deny potential; the social policy of the PiS government is one of the most impressive in Europe.[34] Were Rassemblement National to come to power, their record might be similar; they appear better placed than La France Insoumise (the Mélenchon party). Other national populists are admittedly different, the Spanish Vox party having wealthier supporters.[35] This does not imply support for national populism. As emphasized in Chapter 3, there are other reasons why I do not favour such movements. One reason is that certain welfare policies exclude minority groups, reflecting the discriminatory basis of national populism.[36]

In the British case, it is unlikely that UKIP or the Brexit Party will achieve parliamentary breakthrough, given the obstacles associated with the FPTP system. Under the Johnson leadership, the Conservative Party has nonetheless become more national populist, achieving success among low-income voters in 2019 (see Figure 5.1). This does not guarantee that the Johnson government will be redistributive; the Conservative Party remains popular among businesses and rich citizens. Ideas are also important, many conservatives being ideologically committed to the small state. Despite these caveats, the Johnson government appears to be more redistributive than previous Conservative governments; the 2020 Budget was a watershed.[37]

Some may think it cynical to cast doubt on the potential of new-left parties to change politics. In Britain, there are millions of people, often young and idealistic, who are convinced of the capacity of the new left to reform society in a way which advances the common good. Much of this is commendable. In recent decades, younger citizens have lost out to older counterparts; the former have endured tuition fees and high rents, while the latter have enjoyed booming house prices and protected pensions.[38] Corbynism changed the tone of British politics, bringing these issues to the top of agendas and promoting participation of the young. Youthful idealism has countless achievements which the older dismissed as unpractical; a future new-left government may turn out to be more egalitarian than I anticipate. The capacity of Corbynism to confound 'experts' should not be forgotten.

On the other hand, new-left idealism is related to something distasteful: the tendency for certain supporters to act aggressively towards opponents. Because the new left asserts that its programme is in the interests of the many, some conclude that opponents are inherently selfish. From this conviction, much misconduct results. Certain social media accounts, dealing in abuse and intimidation of opponents, are particularly ugly.

In this chapter, I have attempted to show that the programme of the new left is also associated with self-interest. Elements of new-left agendas may well be inspired by altruism, as is the case with most worldviews, yet the presence of self-interest is unmistakable. This should not surprise us. Self-interest is an unescapable part of the human condition, reflecting shortcomings of reasoning abilities and the influence of structures. If this were to be reflected upon, the sting might be drawn from the views of certain new-left supporters. Some might appreciate that Corbynites are not saints and conservatives are not devils; both are rather human. Such a development would help civilize politics. This is an urgent goal in our partisan society, disfigured by the vilification of opponents.

Notes

1 Jean-Luc Mélenchon is leader of the new-left La France Insoumise party. In the 2017 French presidential election, Mélenchon came fourth with 19.58 per cent of first-round votes. Alberto Garzón is a prominent Spanish left-wing politician. The encounter is related in Spanish in Jesus Maraña (2017) *Al Fondo a la Izquierda*. Barcelona: Planeta; the translation is mine.

2 This chapter also presents definitional challenges. Politicians such as Jeremy Corbyn are described as 'populist', yet this is potentially pejorative. The terms 'socialist' and/or 'social-democratic', favoured by supporters, are problematic for

reasons which I outline in this chapter. 'New left' is a better term; it is non-pejorative and emphasizes differences with older socialists. Though it also refers to a post-war movement (see Michael Kenny (1995) *The First New Left*. London: Lawrence & Wishart), advantages of the term outweigh disadvantages.

3 The changing profile of left-wing support bases is evaluated by Daniel Oesch (2008) 'The Changing Shape of Class Voting: An Individual-Level Analysis of Party Support in Britain, Germany and Switzerland', *European Societies*, 10:3, 329–55; Jane Gingrich and Silja Häusermann (2015) 'The Decline of the Working-Class Vote, the Reconfiguration of the Welfare Support Coalition and Consequences for the Welfare State', *Journal of European Social Policy*, 25:3, 50–75.

4 Research finds that 75 per cent of post-May 2015 Labour members are from ABC1 social grades. The figure for pre-May 2015 Labour members is 76 per cent, indicating a wider issue with social-democratic parties (discussed later in the chapter), Monica Poletti, Tim Bale and Paul Webb (2016) 'Explaining the Pro-Corbyn Surge in Labour's Membership', London School of Economics: European Politics and Policy. Available at: https://blogs.lse.ac.uk/politicsandpolicy/explaining-the-pro-corbyn-surge-in-labours-membership/. Accessed 16 May 2020.

5 Based on analysis of data from Centro de Investigaciones Sociológicas, Jordi Pérez Colomé (2016) 'Podemos es el partido más votado entre las rentas medias y altas'. Available at: www.elpais.com/politica/2016/06/20/actualidad/1466448698_313220.html. Accessed 17 May 2020.

6 Jeff Stein (2016) 'Bernie Sanders's Base isn't the Working Class: It's Young People', *Vox*. Available at: www.vox.com/2016/5/19/11649054/bernie-sanders-working-class-base. Accessed 17 May 2020.

7 The wider programme of the new left is evaluated by Giorgos Charalambous and Gregoris Ioannou (2019) *Left Radicalism and Populism in Europe*. London: Routledge; Chantal Mouffe (2018) *For a Left Populism*. London: Verso Books.

8 Analysis of British Election Study (BES) wave 19 shows this, Edward Fieldhouse, Jane Green, Geoffrey Evans, Jonathan Mellon and Christopher Prosser (2020) *British Election Study Internet Panel Wave 19.*

9 Ray Kiely (2005) 'Capitalist Expansion and the Imperialism–Globalization Debate: Contemporary Marxist Explanations', *Journal of International Relations and Development*, 8:1, 27–57; Robert S. Wistrich (1990) 'Left-Wing Anti-Zionism in Western Societies', in R. S. Wistrich (ed.), *Anti-Zionism and Antisemitism in the Contemporary World*. London: Palgrave Macmillan, 46–52.

10 A modern version is articulated by Aaron Bastani (2019) *Fully Automated Luxury Communism*. New York: Verso Books.

11 Byung-chul Han (2015) 'Why Revolution is no Longer Possible', Open Democracy. Available at: www.opendemocracy.net/en/transformation/why-revolution-is-no-longer-possible/. Accessed 17 May 2020.

12 Costas Panayotakis (2011) *Remaking Scarcity: From Capitalist Inefficiency to Economic Democracy*. London: Pluto.

13 Severin Carell (2014) 'Free Tuition in Scotland Benefits Wealthiest Students the Most – Study', *Guardian*. Available at: www.theguardian.com/education/2014/ apr/ 29/free-tuition-scotland-benefits-wealthiest-students-most-study. Accessed 17 May 2020.

14 Annette Hastings and Peter Matthews (2011) 'Sharp Elbows: Do the Middle-Classes Have Advantages in Public Service Provision and If So How?' Glasgow: University of Glasgow.

15 Torsten Bell (2017) 'For Labour, It's All About What You Say', Resolution Foundation. Available at: www.resolutionfoundation.org/comment/for-labour-its-all-about-what-you-say/. Accessed 16 May 2020.

16 Concerns of the new left are elaborated by Charalambous and Ioannou, *Left Radicalism* and Mouffe, *Left Populism*.

17 Dominik Geering and Silja Häusermann (2013) *Changing Party Electorates and Economic Realignment*. Zurich: Universität Zürich.

18 Core voters are stressed by Gary W. Cox and Mathew D. McCubbins (1986) 'Electoral Politics as a Redistributive Game', *Journal of Politics*, 48, 370–89. Swing voters are emphasized by Assar Lindbeck and Jörgen W. Weibull (1987) 'Balanced-Budget Redistribution as the Outcome of Political Competition', *Public Choice*, 52:3, 273–97.

19 Women Against State Pension Inequality (WASPI) is a group which campaigns against unfair equalization of the state pension age. Labour concessions on WASPI were criticized as regressive, while research shows that richer citizens tend to spend more on train tickets, Oliver Kamm (2019) 'Labour's WASPI Pledge is a Regressive Outrage', CAPX. Available at: www.capx.co/labours-waspi-pledge-is-a-regressive-outrage/. Accessed 17 May 2020; Inequality in Transport (2018) 'What it Costs to Travel'. Available at: www.inequalityintransport.org.uk/exploring-transport-inequality/what-it-costs-travel. Accessed 17 May 2020.

20 Institute for Fiscal Studies (2017) 'General Election Analysis 2017'. Available at: www.ifs.org.uk/uploads/Presentations/Rob%20Joyce%2C%202017%20General%20Election%2C%20manifesto%20analysis.pdf. Accessed 17 May 2020. The Liberal Democrats had the richest support base in this election, demonstrating contingencies of the relationship between support bases and redistribution, yet this is associated with the smaller size of the party.

21 Bell, 'For Labour' is instructive.

22 Institute for Fiscal Studies (2019) 'Party Manifestoes'. Available at: www.ifs.org.uk/election/2019/manifestos. Accessed 17 May 2020.

23 Gingrich and Häusermann, 'Decline'.

24 Cox and McCubbins, 'Electoral Politics'.

25 Walter Scheidel (2018) *The Great Leveler: Violence and the History of Inequality from the Stone Age to the Twenty-First Century*. Princeton: Princeton University Press.

26 James Browne, Cormac O'Dea and David Phillips (2010) 'Personal Tax and Benefit Changes', Institute for Fiscal Studies. Available at: www.ifs.org.uk/budgets/budget2010/browne.pdf. Accessed 17 May 2020.

27 Vivien A. Schmidt (2008) 'Discursive Institutionalism: The Explanatory Power of Ideas and Discourse', *Annual Review of Political Science*, 11:1, 303–26.

28 Robert E. Goodin and Julian Le Grand (2018) *Not Only the Poor: The Middle Classes and the Welfare State*. London: Routledge.

29 Vladimir Lenin (2013) *What is to be Done?* Beijing: Foreign Languages Press.

30 Matthew Smith (2016) 'Election Data Survey Results: 2016 Labour Leadership Election', *Politics and Current Affairs*. Available at: www.d25d2506sfb94s.cloudfront.net/cumulus_ uploads/document/a8ttjtolgq/ElectionDataResults_160923_ FinalCall.pdf. Accessed 17 May 2020.

31 Gingrich and Häusermann, 'Decline'.

32 Colomé, 'Podemos'.

33 Analysis of British Election Study (BES) data is undertaken by John Handley, @jwhandley17, 'Starmer is more popular than Corbyn among both the self-identifying working class and people in lower NS-SEC classes', 16 April 2020. 1.32pm. Tweet. Available at: https://twitter.com/ jwhandley17/status/1250763886938095618. Accessed 4 May 2020.

34 Thomas Prosser and Giga Giorgadze (2018) 'Towards a Theory of Illiberal Dualisation? Conceptualising New Employment and Social Policy Divisions in Poland and the United Kingdom', *Transfer: European Review of Labour and Research*, 24:2, 151–62.

35 Hugo Garrido and Marta Ley (2019) 'El voto de clase sigue existiendo: a menos renta, más votos para el PSOE'. Available at: www.elmundo.es/espana/2019/09/23/ 5d7bd6cafc6c83707e8b45b4.html. Accessed 17 May 2020.

36 Willem De Koster, Peter Achterberg and Jeroen Van der Waal (2013) 'The New Right and the Welfare State: The Electoral Relevance of Welfare Chauvinism and Welfare Populism in the Netherlands', *International Political Science Review*, 34:1, 3–20.

37 Thomas Prosser (2020) 'Budget 2020: Why the Conservatives are Placing More Emphasis on Redistribution', LSE British

Politics and Policy. Available at: https://blogs.lse.ac.uk/politicsandpolicy/budget-2020-redistribution/. Accessed 17 May 2020.

38 Ceryn Evans and Michael Donnelly (2018) 'Deterred by Debt? Young People, Schools and the Escalating Cost of UK Higher Education', *Journal of Youth Studies*, 21:9, 1267–82; Jennifer Hoolachan, Kim McKee, Tom Moore and Adriana Mihael Soaita (2017) '"Generation Rent" and the Ability to "Settle Down": Economic and Geographical Variation in Young People's Housing Transitions', *Journal of Youth Studies*, 20:1, 63–78.

Chapter 6

Is social democracy finished?

The trouble with the social-democratic idea is that it does not stock or sell any of the exciting ideological commodities which totalitarian movements—communist, fascist, or leftist—offer dream-hungry youth. It has no ultimate solution for all human misfortune; it has no prescription for the total salvation of mankind, it cannot promise the firework of the final revolution to settle definitively all the conflict and struggles ... It has an obstinate will to erode by inches the conditions which produce avoidable suffering, oppression, hunger, wars, racial and national hatred, insatiable greed and vindictive envy. (Leszek Kołakowski)[1]

Having evaluated four worldviews, one remains: social democracy. This position seeks compromise between capitalism and socialism, advocating democratic collective action to achieve political and economic freedoms. In the second half of the nineteenth century, pioneers such as Eduard Bernstein rejected efforts to overthrow capitalism by revolution, arguing for a gradualist approach.[2]

Following the end of the Second World War, social-democratic parties assumed power in European countries, introducing reforms which narrowed wealth inequalities and secured lower-class commitment to capitalism. Class compromise was reflected in the support base of social-democratic parties, comprising industrial workers and public sector professionals. Across the West, certain supporters of national populism and the new left claim that their movements are social-democratic. This is problematic, for reasons outlined in relevant chapters; few scholars would place these movements in the social-democratic tradition.

Despite historic ability to reconcile different interests, social democracy is under strain. Across the West, parties such as SPD (Germany), PS (France) and PSOE (Spain) have suffered falls in support (see Figure 6.1); such problems are mirrored in the moderate wing of the British Labour Party, which buckled under new-left challenge. This decline is associated with the failures of governing social democrats. Among right-wingers, recent social-democratic administrations are associated with fiscal indiscipline and high immigration. Among left-wingers, social democrats are criticized for measures which increase inequality.[3]

In this chapter, I examine the potential of social democracy to accommodate the separate interests of today. Notwithstanding the success of the worldview in post-war decades, contemporary challenges are distinct. I am not sure that social democracy can forge

a new class compromise; globalization has sharp-
ened differences in interests. Despite this hesitancy,
I argue that the classic tenets of social democracy, re-
interpreted for the twenty-first century, offer a more
promising means of reconciling different interests than
alternative worldviews. This reflects the credentials
of social democracy as a *governing tactic*. Though a
worldview in its own right, social democracy places
particular emphasis on compromise, adopting the best
elements of other positions. It is even conceivable that
social democracy will outlive social-democratic parties, its ability to compromise influencing alternative
movements.

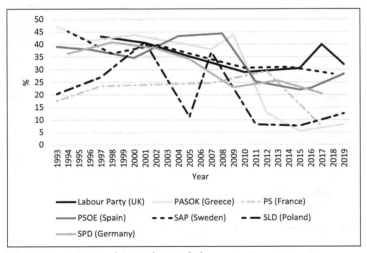

Figure 6.1 Vote share of social-democratic parties in
national elections.

Does social democracy facilitate compromise?

Accommodation of different economic interests is a perennial challenge; viable worldviews must achieve this. A weakness of conservatism is its inability to reconcile self-interest with social stability; inequality associated with conservative economic policies encourages disorder. In Western industrial societies, social democracy has corrected this tendency. This is an explicit aim of social-democratic theory; writers such as Crosland recognized the necessity of capitalist wealth creation,[4] yet advocated redistributive mechanisms to promote fairness and stability. In post-war decades, social democrats took advantage of more accommodating structural conditions to introduce measures which reconciled commercial self-interest with social stability. The British case is famous, Attlee governments developing a welfare state which civilized the country, yet there are examples in other Western countries. Such principles were accepted across the spectrum, ensuring broad societal influence.[5]

Social-democratic economic policies do not entirely avoid the pitfalls associated with conservatism. Given that social democracy advocates a capitalist economic system, albeit one in which there is state intervention, it is inevitable that problems associated with the self-interest of wealthier classes will emerge. This has become more challenging in recent decades. Because of the structural advantages of businesses under globalization, social-democratic governments have made concessions to the rich. This trend occurred across the West from the 1990s and was associated with New Labour. Though it is unfair to draw too great a contrast between these governments and post-war Labour administrations, the former introducing many redistributive policies and the latter implementing certain austere measures, it is true that New Labour made greater cause with the rich. This was partly a structural response to globalization, demonstrated by similar policies in other countries, yet also reflected changing priorities of party elites, associated with estrangement from traditional supporters. Therefore, social democracy does not overcome the economic externalization associated with conservative self-interest, but rather reduces it, success varying between periods.

For new-left supporters, the concessions which social democracy makes to capitalism are reason for rejection. Marxists have long desired the overthrow of capitalism, asserting that defence of the rich is intrinsic to the system. Revolutionary change remains an important part of new-left thought, even if it is now downplayed. The social-democratic response to globalization is seen as a surrender to capitalist rapacity, likely to be more humiliating as capitalism enters its twilight years.[6] I am sceptical of such arguments. Quite aside from difficulties predicting future trajectories of capitalism, events confounding previous attempts, there is the record of Marxist revolutions; these led to political repression and economic inefficiency. Despite the differing conditions which prevail today, involving the sharing economy and automation,[7] institutional overthrow is an excessive gamble. Little good comes from rupture with liberal-democratic institutions; humans behave unpredictably in times of crisis and demagogues tend to capitalize upon resulting instability. For those interested in reconciling diverse interests, it is better to reflect on new ways of achieving class compromise; I advance ideas later in this chapter.

In a globalized world, social democracy has a further advantage over the radical left: it is better placed to appease lower-class attachment to specific places. As I have emphasized, working classes have reacted negatively to globalization; this is associated with the lower skills of these citizens. A historic achievement of social democracy is its ability to accommodate lower class preferences within a broader liberalism.[8] Postwar Labour governments adopted a civic nationalism which reflected the patriotism of working-class supporters; Attlee spoke of a New Jerusalem. This was an exceptional achievement. Though synonymous in the West, liberal and redistributive politics are not natural bedfellows; lower classes prefer societies in which conditions are decent yet tradition prevails.[9] The difficult relationship between the radical left and working classes proves this. There are exceptions in Southern Europe, yet Western Marxists have encountered problems reconciling internationalism and lower-class patriotism.

Despite historic accommodation of liberal and redistributive values, globalization has strained social-democratic coalitions. Because of the increased pace of change, the interests of social democrats of different classes have diverged, endangering class compromise. New Labour fell into this trap, finding immigration particularly troublesome. Mistakes on such issues mean that working-class support for social democracy has declined.

As I write below, this schism might prove fatal for social democracy. On the other hand, there may be a chance for the historic strengths of social democracy to re-emerge.[10] No other worldview has reconciled lower-class interests with liberalism; below I suggest how this might be done again. If this is achieved, it will facilitate a traditional advantage of social democracy: the low-income profile of social-democratic bases. As I have emphasized, movements which aim to redistribute must include the poorest. If the social-democratic relationship with working classes can be regenerated, based on an understanding of lower-class attachment to specific communities, preconditions for redistribution may strengthen.

Social democracy has understood local attachment while limiting the stigmatization of minorities.[11] This is a key weakness of national populism, which blames others and increases internal and external tension. Though social democrats are not entirely innocent of this, previous Labour governments adopting controversial immigration policies, records compare favourably with other movements. Even in contexts in which the radical left has organized large sections of the working class, records have been mixed; French communism was compromised by nationalism.[12] The capacity of social democracy to limit othering means that it remains relevant. We live in an age of blame, in which economic problems are considered the fault of minorities. If social democrats can regain support, based on lines outlined below, the stigmatization of others might be better countered. As limits of blame become apparent, social democracy may regain ground; no other worldview combines economic redistribution and political liberalism, allaying the tensions which promote othering.

This facilitates external stability. As emphasized in Chapter 3, there is a link between internal and external order; national populism, through creation of domestic others, causes international conflict. Aside from the pacifying influence of its internal policies, social democracy is associated with international organizations which promote peace through liberal multilateralism, NATO and the EU being the foremost examples. As with the social-democratic resolution of economic externalization, this response to international externalization is imperfect. Both NATO and the EU have been involved in actions which violate founding principles; the new left has made advanced critiques.[13] Despite these errors, it is unwise to advocate dissolution; such institutions have underwritten decades of peace and isolationism is dangerous.[14] Social democrats should engage with such organizations with a renewed vigour, working to address shortcomings. In the case of the EU, economic policy and freedom of movement require serious reflection, prevailing approaches causing crises. Though reform will be difficult, it is vital that social democrats continue engagement with international partners.

What next?

Social democrats have made mistakes; certain errors reflect ideological faults, as opposed to ones of implementation. Given such mistakes, some may conclude that critics of social democracy deserve their chance. This is consistent with the view that political philosophies fall out of fashion. According to this perspective, social democracy has run out of steam, as occurs when worldviews dominate for a long period.[15] And social democracy has had a long run. Maturing after the Second World War, the movement played a key role in the shaping of European society. As recently as the early 2000s, most major European countries were governed by social democrats.

The problem is that alternative worldviews are associated with tension between self-interest and the common good. Though social democracy is far from perfect, as I note above, it *better* reconciles different interests than other positions. Given the propensity of alternative worldviews to create externalities, particularly marked in the case of national populism, positions based on compromise may soon re-emerge. The example of the 1930s is illustrative. Though social democracy underwent decline in this decade, related to the rise of extremism, the failings of radical worldviews paved the way for post-war renewal.[16]

There are barriers to another renaissance. As I have stressed, globalization has created differences in the interests of social-democratic support bases. If social democracy is to endure, it is vital that it reconciles the interests of poorer and richer supporters. Here I see two issues.

Firstly, social democracy must reconcile itself to lower-class attachment to place. The resistance of lower-class citizens to change is rooted in their inferior mobility; these citizens have more capital sunk in specific localities and, in a globalized world, are particularly sensitive to overhaul of local conditions. In recent decades, social democrats have failed to appreciate this attachment; in the case of immigration, such opposition has been dismissed as bigotry. This is associated with the more privileged profile of social-democratic elites. Because they tend to be wealthier and more educated, these politicians have misunderstood lower-class concerns.

It is vital that social democrats reconnect with such concerns. There are undoubted examples of intolerance among such citizens, yet it is unrealistic to argue that *all* resistance to immigration is bigoted. As I have written, such opposition often reflects lower-class interests. Given that the historic strength of social democracy is the fulfilment of lower-class demands within the existing system, it is imperative that social democrats take such concerns seriously. In spheres such as industrial policy and immigration, continuity of local conditions might be emphasized.

Policymakers should not be ashamed of paying particular attention to the needs of long-term residents. Because of the greater capital which such citizens have bound up in these communities, they have a larger stake in their future. Immigration should occur at levels which are acceptable to residents. I would not advocate the Danish example, in which social democrats adopted a hard-line immigration policy and regained working-class votes, yet it suggests the importance of engagement with voter concerns; liberal social democrats might find enlightened variants. This issue is not necessarily related to ethnicity; many ethnic minority citizens, themselves long-term residents of particular communities, desire secure borders. There must also be initiatives which provide decent employment. In the British case, regional policy should improve conditions in places such as Ebbw Vale. Regional development was more advanced in post-war decades, yet has progressively deteriorated; Britain now has the worst regional inequality in Western Europe.[17]

Secondly, social democrats must pay attention to the relative position of specific groups. A paradox is that electorates are sensitive to marginal rates of economic growth, rather than absolute levels. In the British case, the contrast between post-war decades and the previous decade is instructive. Even though the average Briton is richer than her grandparents, she tends to be less satisfied with politics.[18] This is associated with differing levels of marginal growth. In post-war years, there were marked improvements in living standards; in recent years, advances have been slow. This is not only a British phenomenon; it has occurred across developed countries.[19] The relative position of particular groups is also crucial. Historically, the position of upper-working classes and lower-middle classes is significant; these citizens are sensitive to declines in status and tend to be politically organized. Recent experiences are consistent with this, such groups embracing anti-establishment parties.[20]

Social democrats must address these issues. Though such challenges are associated with debates about inequality, the focus of sustained attention, they are distinctive and concern self-interest; the tendency of humans to react badly to negative marginal changes is based on their dislike of losing social position. There are difficulties addressing such structural challenges, dealt with below, yet mere awareness of this issue will be useful. If policymakers recognize a problem, the concern tends to become mainstreamed.[21] There are specific measures which could be adopted. Not only might there be periodic review of changes to incomes, but tax and social security policy could be designed in a way which balances gains among different groups.

Such issues are wider than one party. In advocating social-democratic renaissance, I am most concerned with the broader influence of the worldview. The thirty years which followed the Second World War are a model. Social-democratic parties were frequently in office, yet wider acceptance of principles was the greater achievement; conservatives became committed Keynesians. I envisage a role for a moderate Labour Party, but am more concerned that rival parties and institutions adopt social-democratic principles. Related international trends are also vital; global social-democratic success underpinned the post-war consensus.[22]

Introduction of suggested measures is nonetheless difficult. This is because challenges to social democracy, such as mass migration and deindustrialization, reflect structural pressures; we know this because they have occurred across countries, largely irrespective of government policy. The post-war consensus reflected kinder structural conditions, including international economic coordination and tighter borders. Such constraints are often overlooked by policymakers and media, though have long been recognized by scholars.[23] It is important that I make this point; throughout this book, I have emphasized the importance of structures and limitations of ideas. This implies that humans have restricted ability to shape future events, meaning that political action achieves limited effects. When writing a previous book,[24] in which I advanced proposals with a similar caveat, a colleague warned me that this was a melancholic way to present ideas.

I disagree with this premise. It is the task of politicians to market policies; scholars should depict the world as they perceive it. The poor ageing of many proposals in academic books, authors underestimating structural constraints, warns against undue optimism. Despite the importance of realism, we need not be fatalistic; real changes introduced by previous generations show that human influence is sometimes decisive. Recent trends, involving popular rebellions such as Brexit and a fashion for reregulation, imply that systemic changes are underway. COVID-19 may also have weakened globalization, heralding limits on movement of people and capital. When existing systems are eroding, opportunities for action expand; critical juncture theory reminds us of this.[25] In previous critical junctures, such as periods following the end of the Second World War and the fall of communism, politicians initiated profound change. Developments may not go the way of social democrats, yet rare chances to implement systemic change are at least emerging. Given the historic successes of social democracy, the worldview is well placed to capitalize upon opportunities. Reconciliation of redistributive and liberal politics may be a historic curiosity,[26] yet Western countries have been moulded in this cast. If we follow the theory of path dependency, which states that societies tend to return to tried methods, future attempts may have higher chance of success.

It may be that social democracy does not weather its current crisis. The divisions which exist in the movement will not be easy to overcome. Though there has always been tension between poorer and richer parts of social-democratic electorates, such divides are increasingly unbridgeable; current difficulties of the

Labour Party, involving tension between the so-called Hartlepool and Hampstead wings, are telling. The collapse of social democracy cannot be ruled out.

If social democracy does wither as a political force, the survival of its broader programme is imperative. Social-democratic principles do not necessarily require formal parties. Given that such values fulfil basic societal needs, institutions sometimes naturally reflect them. The Polish case is instructive. Though there is no formal social-democratic party within the country, politics divided into national-populist and liberal camps, social-democratic values are influential. Social policies have been designed on such lines; former Prime Minister Donald Tusk, leader of the economic libertarian Platforma Obywatelska (PO) party, spoke of his conversion to interventionism.[27]

It may be that another movement considered in this book assumes a social-democratic form; certain supporters of new-left and national-populist parties affirm the social-democratic credentials of their causes. Though I disagree that this is the case, it might be that such movements come to resemble social-democratic parties. Stranger things have happened. Such a process may be driven by the compromises which power makes inevitable. Modern social democracy evolved from radical nineteenth-century labour movements, the experience of governing smoothing rough edges.

A wider challenge to the politics of compromise is the survival of liberal democracy itself. Recent polls show disenchantment with democracy; a 2018 survey showed that only 51 per cent of Americans have faith in it.[28] This is worrying as liberal democracy promotes the balancing of interests; universal suffrage ensures recognition of voter preferences, reflecting wisdom-of-crowd-type principles, while deliberative institutions, such as parliaments and presses, allow balanced debate.[29] Problems such as inequality and corruption indicate need for reform, yet alternatives are less able to reconcile different interests. Non-democratic regimes have advantages, including capacity to plan and implement decisions, yet are famously insensitive to popular concerns, reflecting a lack of voice-giving institutions.

Though approval of non-democratic systems is troubling, a more immediate threat to liberal democracy is the rise of direct expressions of interest. In recent years, institutions such as referendums and social media have become more influential, reflecting cynicism with established politics.[30] These developments do not weaken the democratic aspects of liberal democracy, quite the opposite, yet they strain deliberative institutions. Recent innovations bypass deliberative forums, using blunt forms of expression and undermining careful negotiation of different interests. Social media is particularly bad. Exposing citizens primarily to views of their own side, it encourages demonization of opponents. Talk of the end of liberal democracy may be exaggerated, liberal-democratic institutions having deep roots, yet such developments are worrying. The least that can be said is that we live in a direct and polarized age, characterized by institutions which promote abrasive expressions of interest.

As emphasized in this book, such language is not productive; politics should attempt to balance different interests. Faced with such challenges, there is a need for the strengthening of deliberative institutions, albeit reformed ones. This involves multiple challenges,[31] yet reflection on self-interest is fruitful; recognition that we are self-interested involves concession that separate interests are legitimate, implying the need for adjudication. Structural trends are admittedly discouraging, as I note above, yet recent developments should not make us resigned. Trends can reverse quickly. As problems with direct participation become apparent, deliberative alternatives may become more appealing.

Why understanding self-interest is vital

In my opinion, renewal of social democracy within a liberal-democratic framework, built on historic strengths but adapted to meet challenges of the twenty-first century, better reconciles different interests than alternatives. Two qualifications are necessary. Firstly, this way forward is based on my reading of contemporary politics. Given that I have emphasized the imperfections of human reasoning, I can scarcely claim that these are all the challenges faced by twenty-first-century humanity. My arguments necessarily reflect the point of view of a particular person in a particular place. The solutions I have proposed, answering identified problems, reflect this. My hope for this book is that it initiates dialogue; others will have different perspectives and I am interested in these.

Related to this is a second qualification. As they have progressed through this work, many readers will have reflected upon my own self-interest. I can scarcely complain. The premise of this book is that humans are self-interested and that this manifests itself politically. In my defence, I have done my best to be sensitive to this issue and, contrary to constructionists, consider that objective analysis is sometimes possible. My advocacy of a renewed social democracy, delivering collective benefits and stability, is based on this ambition. I am also an individual; as I have emphasized, individuals are less constrained than groups.

This is nonetheless to avoid the main point; I am necessarily self-interested. In terms of my advocacy of social democracy, I come from the groups which have benefited from the worldview; not only are my family of working-class stock, but my academic job places me in the social-democratic middle class. I am also a white, heterosexual male. I do not accept that this invalidates my right to discuss certain issues, as some assert,[32] yet this status is undoubtedly relevant. Race and gender have a crucial influence on outlooks; were my identity different, I would understand the world otherwise.

I am aware that a series of weaknesses of Western social democracy overlap with my own interests. One limitation is lack of serious engagement with development issues. As Westerners often forget, much of the world lives in precarity and want. In the same way as the new left are sometimes inattentive to those on low incomes, social democrats can be unconcerned with these issues, paying lip service to development yet failing to dedicate political capital. I can scarcely exclude myself from this. Though this book is concerned with developed countries, the fact that I am interested in these contexts is a form of reconciliation with the international status quo. For those who live in extreme poverty, rupture with existing institutions may be more appealing.

I also did not consider environmental issues. Given that climate change poses an existential threat, many will judge this short-sighted. Damage to the environment is a key externality which arises from self-interest and is particularly associated with conservatism, which advocates deregulation, and national populism, the anti-elitism of which can prompt climate denial. Though my focus in this work was not the environment, an inability to mainstream environmental issues is a major failure of researchers. For too long, the environment has been treated as an afterthought, rather than a global emergency. The emergence of Greta Thunberg has provided a welcome jolt.

In fairness to me, it can be argued that political stability, based on reconciliation of different interests, is a precondition to the resolution of developmental and environmental issues. Effective management of these areas requires global regulation which encompasses diverse stakeholders, the complexity of which is unprecedented.[33] If we understand each other better, recognizing that different perspectives are legitimate rather than pathological, it will be easier to reach international agreements.

In radical circles, particularly in the United States, it is fashionable to ask others to 'check your privilege!'. This is based on the idea that identity is bound up with political opinion and is primarily asked of the 'privileged', i.e. white, richer citizens. Though I cannot agree that opinion is a straight function of identity, nor with the associated disapproval of 'privileged' opining on minority affairs, the phrase at least invites self-reflection; this is no bad thing in an age which is characterized by a tendency to blame others.

In this spirit, I suggest that people might reflect on the link between their outlook and interests. This is not to imply, à la a revivalist preacher, that we are incurably depraved; as I have emphasized, humans are also capable of altruism. I rather suggest that there is a persistent link between self-interest and preferences, inherent in all worldviews, even those which are sometimes thought free of this. I suspect that few will assert that their politics are free of self-interest; the impulse is too human. Given this is the case, I invite reflection; some may be surprised by the results.

Many will have disagreed with my ideas; this is inevitable and I welcome it. I nonetheless hope that critics agree that self-interest is a crucial topic of debate. For too long, many have ignored or stylized this vital issue. In writing this book, my goal has been to draw attention to this subject; others might elaborate different problems or alternative means of reconciliation, working with themes which I have overlooked. We are living in a world in which key groups are at odds with one another; this trend occurs across countries, being long-standing in the United States,[34] and is highly concerning. There are many ways of addressing this crisis, yet reflection on self-interest is one; it leads to better understanding of ourselves and others. We will never escape self-interest, yet awareness means that we gain a modicum of control. Recognition and taming of basic impulses, the principle upon which civilization is founded, surely improves us.

Notes

1 Leszek Kołakowski (1982) 'What is Living (and what is Dead) in the Social-Democratic Idea?', *Encounter*, 58, 11.
2 Eduard Bernstein (1961) *Evolutionary Socialism: A Criticism and Affirmation*. New York: Schocken Books; Ben Jackson (2013) 'Social Democracy', in M. Freeden, L. T. Sargent and M. Stears (eds), *The Oxford Handbook of Political Ideologies*. Oxford: Oxford University Press, 348–63.
3 Contemporary accounts equate social-democratic decline with austerity and immigration, e.g. David Bailey, Jean-Michel de Waele, Fabien Escalona and Mathieu Vieira (eds) (2016) *European Social Democracy During the Global Economic Crisis*. Manchester: Manchester University Press; Ashley Lavelle (2016) *The Death of Social Democracy: Political Consequences in the 21st Century*. London: Routledge; Carly Elizabeth Schall (2016) *The Rise*

and Fall of the Miraculous Welfare Machine: Immigration and Social Democracy in Twentieth-Century Sweden. New York: Cornell University Press. Older literature discusses causes of crises of the 1980s and early 1990s; these factors remain relevant and include the breakdown of the Keynesian consensus, changes in socio-economic structures and onset of postmaterial politics. See Ronald Inglehart (1977) *The Silent Revolution: Changing Values and Political Styles among Western Publics.* Princeton: Princeton University Press; Wolfgang Merkel (1991) 'After the Golden Age: Is Social Democracy Doomed to Decline?', in C. Lemke and G. Marks (eds), *The Crisis of Socialism in Europe.* Durham, NC: Duke University Press; Jonas Pontusson (1995) 'Explaining the Decline of European Social Democracy: The Role of Structural Economic Change', *World Politics*, 47:4, 502–33; Georg Vobruba (1983) *Politik mit dem Wohlfahrtsstaat.* Frankfurt: Suhrkamp, 136.

4 Anthony Crosland (2013) *The Future of Socialism.* New edition with foreword by Gordon Brown. London: Constable Publishing.

5 Nicholas Timmins (2001) *The Five Giants: A Biography of the Welfare State.* New York: HarperCollins.

6 Wolfgang Streeck (2016) *How Will Capitalism End? Essays on a Failing System.* New York: Verso Books.

7 Serhat Koloğlugil (2015) 'Digitizing Karl Marx: The New Political Economy of General Intellect and Immaterial Labour', *Rethinking Marxism*, 27:1, 123–37.

8 Thomas Meyer and Lewis Hinchman (2007) *The Theory of Social Democracy.* Cambridge: Polity.

9 A relationship between support for economic redistribution and cultural conservatism is shown by Ariel Malka, Yphtach Lelkes and Christopher J. Soto (2017) 'Are Cultural and Economic Conservatism Positively Correlated? A Large-Scale Cross-National Test', *British Journal of Political Science*, 49:3, 1–25.

10 Interesting ideas are offered by Claire Ainsley (2018) *The New Working Class: How to Win Hearts, Minds and Votes.* Bristol: Policy Press.

11 Meyer and Hinchman, *Theory of Social Democracy*, 191–205.

12 Irwin M. Wall (1977) 'The French Communists and the Algerian War', *Journal of Contemporary History*, 12:3, 521–43.

13 Noam Chomsky (2008) 'Humanitarian Imperialism: The New Doctrine of Imperial Right', *Monthly Review*, 60:4, 22–5.

14 Stephen Van Evera (1998) 'Offense, Defense, and the Causes of War', *International Security*, 22:4, 5–43.

15 Diminishing returns of social democracy, associated with increasing wealth of the electorate, are emphasized by Karl Loxbo, Jonas Hinnfors, Magnus Hagevi, Sofie Blombäck and Marie Demker (2019) 'The Decline of Western European Social Democracy: Exploring the Transformed Link between Welfare State Generosity and the Electoral Strength of Social Democratic Parties, 1975–2014', *Party Politics*. Online First. Available at: https://journals.sagepub.com/doi/full/10.1177/1354068819861339.

16 Tony Judt (2006) *Postwar: A History of Europe since 1945*. New York: Penguin, ch. 11.

17 Inequality Briefing (2015) 'Briefing 61: Regional Inequality in the UK is the Worst in Western Europe'. Available at www.inequalitybriefing.org/brief/briefing-61-regional-inequality-in-the-uk-is-the-worst-in-western-europe. Accessed 17 May 2020.

18 Russell J. Dalton (2004) *Democratic Challenges, Democratic Choices: The Erosion of Political Support in Advanced Industrial Democracies*. Oxford: Oxford University Press; Paul Whiteley, Harold D. Clarke, David Sanders and Marianne Stewart (2016) 'Why Do Voters Lose Trust in Governments? Public Perceptions of Government Honesty and Trustworthiness in Britain 2000–2013', *The British Journal of Politics and International Relations*, 18:1, 234–54.

19 Roger Eatwell and Matthew Goodwin (2018) *National Populism: The Revolt against Liberal Democracy*. London: Pelican, 212–14.

20 Daniel Oesch (2008) 'Explaining Workers' Support for Right-Wing Populist Parties in Western Europe: Evidence

from Austria, Belgium, France, Norway, and Switzerland', *International Political Science Review*, 29:3, 349–73.

21 Teresa Rees (1998) *Mainstreaming Equality in the European Union: Education, Training and Labour Market Policies.* London: Routledge.

22 Judt, *Postwar*, ch. 11.

23 Stephen Marglin and Juliet B. Schor (1991) *The Golden Age of Capitalism: Reinterpreting the Post War Experience.* Oxford: Oxford University Press.

24 Thomas Prosser (2018) *European Labour Movements in Crisis: From Indecision to Indifference.* Manchester: Manchester University Press.

25 Giovanni Capoccia and R. Daniel Kelemen (2007) 'The Study of Critical Junctures: Theory, Narrative, and Counterfactuals in Historical Institutionalism', *World Politics*, 59:3, 341–69.

26 Malka et al., 'Cultural and Economic Conservatism'.

27 Michał Wąsowski (2014) 'Tusk przeprasza za to, że chciał obniżać podatki. Kiedyś mówił: "Kieszeń podatnika jest nadmiernie obciążona"'. Available at: www.natemat.pl/100997,tusk-kiedys-chcial-obnizac-podatki. Accessed 17 May 2020.

28 Kim Hart (2018) 'Exclusive Poll: Only Half of Americans Have Faith in Democracy', *Axios*. Available at: www.axios.com/poll-americans-faith-in-democracy-2e94a938-4365-4e80-9fb6-d9743d817710.html. Accessed 17 May 2020.

29 Yascha Mounk (2018) *The People vs. Democracy: Why Our Freedom is in Danger and How to Save it.* Cambridge, MA: Harvard University Press.

30 Mounk, *The People vs. Democracy*.

31 Several authorities discuss strategies for the reform of liberal democracy, e.g. Patrick J. Deneen (2018) *Why Liberalism Failed.* Connecticut: Yale University Press; Alessandro Ferrara (2018) 'Can Political Liberalism Help Us Rescue "the People" from Populism?', *Philosophy & Social Criticism*, 44:4, 463–77; Mark Lilla (2018) *The Once and Future Liberal: After Identity Politics.* Oxford: Oxford University Press; Mounk, *The People vs. Democracy*; Adrian Pabst (2019) *The Demons of Liberal Democracy.* Cambridge: Polity Press.

32 Reni Eddo-Lodge (2018) *Why I'm No Longer Talking to White People about Race*. London: Bloomsbury.

33 Thomas G. Weiss, Ramesh Thakur and John Gerard Ruggie (2010) *Global Governance and the UN: An Unfinished Journey*. Indiana: Indiana University Press.

34 Jonathan Haidt (2012) *The Righteous Mind: Why Good People are Divided by Politics and Religion*. New York: Random House.

Appendix

Devising a future research agenda

Some remarks on the purpose of this appendix are necessary. As I outline in the main text, this is not a purely academic book; it is one aimed at the academic–popular 'crossover' market. Given this orientation, it would have been inappropriate to have burdened the main text with detailed engagement with academic literature. In this appendix, I outline a programme for future academic research, comprising analysis of (1) relative deprivation and the evolution of worldviews, (2) synergies between ideas and interests, and (3) the relationship between support bases and redistributive outcomes. The breadth of this agenda implies that I cannot undertake this work myself, yet there are specific questions which interest me; I indicate where this is the case.

It is necessary to provide more information on my background. I am a Reader (Associate Professor) in European social policy at Cardiff University. I specialize in employment and social policy and political economy, fields predicated on institutional theory, and have published extensively in these areas.[1] My most significant academic publication is a book: *European Labour Movements in Crisis*. This was published by Manchester University Press in 2018 and argues that the support bases of European trade unions and social-democratic parties promote competitive behaviour. My current research examines the relationship between party support bases and socio-economic policies; this is elaborated below.

(1) Relative deprivation and the evolution of worldviews

As argued in the main text, relative changes in socio-economic conditions are particularly important, often predicting satisfaction better than absolute measures. Relative deprivation theory has a long history. Garry Runciman developed the theory in the 1960s, elaborating preconditions to relative deprivation and inter and intra-group forms. The approach continues to inspire investigation; there have been recent studies of relative deprivation and emotion,[2] culture[3] and trajectories of change.[4]

Despite this work, there has been limited investigation of relative deprivation and the evolution of worldviews. National populism is an exception. Given that national populism has thrived in rich countries such as Austria, the Netherlands and Switzerland, scholars acknowledge the importance of relative changes.[5] Findings of many studies are nonetheless ambiguous.

Not only is the relationship between unemployment and support for the radical right unclear,[6] but studies find a weak link between relative deprivation and support for such parties. Recent research has nonetheless adopted refined criteria, identifying new relationships between economic conditions and support for national populism. Analysing the European Social Survey, Rooduijn and Burgoon contend that 'economic hardship leads to radical right voting when the socioeconomic circumstances are favourable, and to radical left voting when net migration is modest'.[7]

This literature is an example for scholarship on conservatism and social democracy, which has been slower to conceptualize relative changes. In the case of conservatism, there is need for work which establishes the relationship between conservative economic policies and relative deprivation. Though recent studies associate relative increases in inequality with violent conflict,[8] there is limited new work. Scholars might evaluate marginal deprivation in areas which are the subject of conservative deregulation; these include benefit and minimum wage levels and access to housing. Using quantitative analysis, scholars might test relationships with disorder; specific dependent variables include crime, protest and strike levels.

In the case of social democracy, there is need for work which examines relationships between relative deprivation and social-democratic decline. Several groups might be studied; demographics such as skilled and semi-skilled manual occupations, public-sector workers and cultural professionals are crucial to social-democratic coalitions. Indicators of relative deprivation which are relevant to these groups must be devised; these might include real wage growth, household income and access to housing. This analysis would primarily be quantitative, yet qualitative study could investigate the reaction of social-democratic parties to these issues. Such examinations of conservatism and social democracy should also adopt cross-national research designs; this is a strength of literature on national populism and allows for fine-grained analysis.

(2) Understanding synergies between ideas and interests

As I emphasize in the text, there is much work on the sociology of knowledge. Following sociologists cited in the main text, primarily Mannheim but also Marx and Durkheim, subsequent scholars have developed this field. Peter L. Berger and Thomas Luckmann are influential. In *The Social Construction of Reality*, Berger and Luckmann distinguish between 'objective reality', codified within institutions and stocks of knowledge, and the quotidian manner in which humans interpret this reality.[9] Consequent work has emphasized the construction of ideas. Inspired by Michel Foucault,[10] who argued that discourse constituted reality, sociologists of knowledge have paid attention to discursive constructions. The sociology of knowledge approach to discourse (SKAD), a contemporary framework popular within German academia, is a prime example.[11] This approach combines insights of Berger and Luckmann and Foucault, considering 'the knowledge side and the "power effects of discourses", the infrastructures of discourse production as well as the institutional effects and "external" impacts on practice emerging out of discourses meeting fields of practices'.

A modern case discussed in the text, feminism and its association with capitalism, has inspired extensive literature on linkages between feminist ideas and economic imperatives; Nancy Fraser is a key authority,[12] theorizing broader associations, yet there are case studies which demonstrate specific relationships.[13] This work indicates ways forward for other literatures. An issue which is discussed extensively in this book, the relationship between national-populist and liberal ideas and the economic status of proponents, could be the subject of more attention. Though there are multiple studies of causes of national populism, engagement with systemic explanations might be stronger. Limited attention is paid to triangulation between worldviews, mobility and economic needs. Though edited volumes develop such explanations, Kriesi et al. stressing exit options of educated citizens,[14] there are no monographs which analyze long-term trends in political economy.

Taking inspiration from scholarship on feminism and capitalism, work might interrogate broad synergies between liberalism and/or national populism and mobility and economic needs, based on recent insights of sociology of knowledge. There is scope for book-length studies which chart historic development of such relationships. This agenda would be buttressed by empirical investigation. There is work which operationalizes mobility, studies examining the relationship between mobility and Brexit voting,[15] yet more is needed.

Interesting independent variables might be devised, including capacity to relocate, proximity of kin and time spent in localities. Dependent variables would include preferences associated with liberalism and national populism, such as support for the death penalty and attitudes to immigration. As emphasized in Chapter 4, I am interested in whether the mobility of educated liberals affects preferences. This is difficult to establish, as is the question of how mobility affects business behaviour, yet qualitative study could be elucidative. Such work might involve detailed interviews with policymakers, establishing whether mobility had influenced decision making.

Systemic challenges to liberalism mean that re-thinking of the worldview is imperative. Though some contend that liberalism is finished,[16] lack of plausible alternatives means that most are keen to discuss reforms. Scholars emphasize the need for focus on socio-economic grievances which underpin populism,[17] rejection of identity politics[18] and domestication of nationalism.[19] Though such ideas are diverse, there seems to be agreement that liberalism should reconnect with traditional constituents. The studies which

I suggest would help this agenda, refining theories of the relationship between liberal ideas and interests and providing evidence for those who wish to reform liberalism.

(3) Conceptualizing the relationship between support bases and redistribution

The question which is the subject of Chapter 5, whether economic equality can be achieved with wealthy support bases, has inspired limited direct debate. This is because the phenomenon of left-wing parties with affluent support bases is new. As I emphasize in the text, this issue has resonance beyond the British new left. Not only are new-left parties in other countries touched by the problem, but social democrats are also affected, working-class voters leaving the Labour Party prior to the Corbyn leadership. Given the relevance of this problem, research will yield crucial insight into the future of redistributive politics.

There is some existing work. Scholars have long noticed wealthy supporters of left-wing parties,[20] reflecting factors such as the decline of the traditional working class. As this phenomenon has become more acute, researchers have investigated implications for redistribution. In analysis of statements during election campaigns, Geering and Häusermann find that left-wing parties with wealthier bases tend to remain committed to redistribution.[21] This study nonetheless uses data from the early 2000s, the problem subsequently worsening. Recent investigation is less optimistic. In a study of European countries, Gingrich and Häusermann show that left-wing governments with strong working-class support provide more generous unemployment benefits than those with richer support bases.

In future years, there is need for further investigation of the relationship between support bases and redistribution, reflecting growing importance of this issue. I am involved in this. In a funding bid which is in preparation, colleagues and I propose study of social-democratic and new-left parties in European countries. Using quantitative and qualitative techniques, we will investigate the constraining influence of support bases; this is not only politically interesting, but will allow us to reach wider conclusions about the relevance of structures and ideas.

Successful quantitative analysis hinges on the preparation of robust dependent variables. General measures of socio-economic equality are too crude; variables must be devised which directly reflect party influence. Such variables will be constructed based on data from party manifestos. In the UK, the IFS undertakes analysis of the fiscal implications of each of the parties' spending plans, assessing outcomes by income decile. Similar data exist in other European countries, allowing compilation of pan-European data on redistribution.

There is scope for analysis of manifestos. The Manifesto Project evaluates party positions on issues such as 'welfare state', 'labour groups' and 'social ownership', with data from multiple European countries. Such variables permit studies evaluating European trends, yet they are not bespoke and there are no regional data. To address these shortcomings, we will undertake analysis of regional manifestos in Germany and Spain. Strong regional governance in these countries lends itself to such analysis; well-resourced regional parties produce detailed manifestoes and regular elections provide large sample size. Variables specific to our interests will be devised, evaluating positions on issues such as 'public housing policy', 'unemployment benefits' and 'student policy'. This will allow intra-country studies of Germany and Spain.

The socio-economic profiles of party support bases will be our independent variables. Though support bases can be defined in terms of voters, members or activists, we are particularly interested in voters; they tend to be most influential.[22] Data are available on support bases across European countries, much of which have been the subject of academic analysis,[23] even if the extent of these data differ between countries. Based on such sources, we will develop independent variables reflecting groups which are most important to parties.

We will also conduct qualitative research; given limitations of quantitative methods, such analysis will allow appreciation of strategic and ideational influences in specific cases. Research in Germany, Poland, Spain and the UK will be undertaken; these countries are representative of others and exhibit variance in key independent variables. We shall evaluate changing party strategies, assessing the relationship with support bases. We will also study the nature of party discourses. Consistent with research on the power of ideas,[24] certain discourses may become prevalent within parties, allowing circumvention of structural constraints.

We plan to study specific policy areas. Given that certain fields are preoccupations of particular classes, low-income citizens being especially concerned with issues such as social housing and benefits, we will analyse the extent to which parties prioritize such issues. Qualitative analysis will be based on documentary analysis and semi-structured research interviews with party elites, allowing for careful tracking of the extent to which discourse and party strategies have changed with support bases and reflect historic traditions. Additional qualitative research at regional level within the countries, particularly feasible within Germany and Spain given strong regional institutions, will complement national-level data.

Notes

1 Thomas Prosser (2016) 'Economic Union without Social Union: The Strange Case of the European Social Dialogue', *Journal of European Social Policy*, 26:5, 460–72; Thomas Prosser (2017) 'Explaining Implementation through Varieties of Capitalism Theory: The Case of the Telework and Work-Related Stress Agreements', *Journal of Common Market Studies*, 55:4, 889–908.

2 Danny Osborne and Chris G. Sibley (2015) 'Opposing Paths to Ideology: Group-Based Relative Deprivation Predicts Conservatism through Warmth toward Ingroup and Outgroup Members', *Social Justice Research*, 28:1, 27–51.

3 Kees Van den Bos, Tanja S. Van Veldhuizen and Al K. C. Au (2015) 'Counter Cross-Cultural Priming and Relative Deprivation: The Role of Individualism–Collectivism', *Social Justice Research*, 28:1, 52–75.

4 Roxane De la Sablonniere, Francine Tougas, Donald M. Taylor, Jonathan Crush, David McDonald and Radchenko Onon Perenlei (2015) 'Social Change in Mongolia and South Africa: The Impact of Relative Deprivation Trajectory and Group Status on Well-Being and Adjustment to Change', *Social Justice Research*, 28:1, 102–22.

5 Cas Mudde and Cristóbal Rovira Kaltwasser (2018) 'Studying Populism in Comparative Perspective: Reflections on the Contemporary and Future Research Agenda', *Comparative Political Studies*, 51:13, 1667–93.

6 For conflicting accounts see Kai Arzheimer (2009) 'Contextual Factors and the Extreme Right Vote in Western Europe, 1980–2002', *American Journal of Political Science*, 53, 259–75; Robert W. Jackman and Karin Volpert (1996) 'Conditions Favouring Parties of the Extreme Right in Western Europe', *British Journal of Political Science*, 26:1, 501–21; Duane Swank and Hans-Georg Betz (2003) 'Globalization, the Welfare State and Right-Wing Populism in Western Europe', *Socio-Economic Review*, 1:2, 215–45.

7 Matthijs Rooduijn and Brian Burgoon (2018) 'The Paradox of Wellbeing: Do Unfavourable Socioeconomic and Sociocultural Contexts Deepen or Dampen Radical Left and Right Voting among the Less Well-Off?', *Comparative Political Studies*, 51:13, 1720–53.

8 Nemanja Džuverovic (2013) 'Does More (or Less) Lead to Violence? Application of the Relative Deprivation Hypothesis on Economic Inequality-Induced Conflicts', *Croatian International Relations Review*, 19:68, 53–72.

9 Peter L. Berger and Thomas Luckmann (1996) *The Social Construction of Reality: A Treatise in the Sociology of Knowledge*. New York: Garden City.

10 Michel Foucault (1990) *The History of Sexuality: An Introduction, Volume I*. New York: Vintage; Michel Foucault (2012) *Discipline and Punish: The Birth of the Prison*. New York: Vintage.

11 Reiner Keller (2011) 'The Sociology of Knowledge Approach to Discourse (SKAD)', *Human Studies*, 34:1, 43–45.

12 Nancy Fraser (2013) 'Feminism, Capitalism, and the Cunning of History', in *Fortunes of Feminism: From State-Managed Capitalism to Neoliberal Crisis*. London: Verso, 209–27.

13 Adrienne Roberts (2012) 'Financial Crisis, Financial Firms … and Financial Feminism? The Rise of "Transnational Business Feminism" and the Necessity of Marxist-Feminist IPE', *Socialist Studies*, 8:2, 85–108.

14 Hanspeter Kriesi, Edgar Grande, Romain Lachat, Martin Dolezal, Simon Bornschier and Timotheos Frey (2008) *West European Politics in the Age of Globalization*. Cambridge: Cambridge University Press.

15 Tak Wing Chan, Morag Henderson, Maria Sironi and Juta Kawalerowicz (2017) 'Understanding the Social and Cultural Bases of Brexit', Department of Quantitative Social Science, University College London; Neil Lee, Katy Morris and Thomas Kemeny (2018) 'Immobility and the Brexit Vote', *Cambridge Journal of Regions, Economy and Society*, 11:1, 143–63.

16 Patrick J. Deneen (2018) *Why Liberalism Failed*. Connecticut: Yale University Press.

17 Alessandro Ferrara (2018) 'Can Political Liberalism Help Us Rescue "the People" from Populism?', *Philosophy & Social Criticism*, 44:4, 463–77.

18 Mark Lilla (2018) *The Once and Future Liberal: After Identity Politics*. Oxford: Oxford University Press.

19 Yascha Mounk (2018) *The People vs. Democracy: Why Our Freedom is in Danger and How to Save it*. Cambridge, MA: Harvard University Press.

20 Ronald Inglehart (1977) *The Silent Revolution: Changing Values and Political Styles among Western Publics*. Princeton: Princeton University Press; Daniel Oesch (2008) 'The Changing Shape of Class Voting: An Individual-Level Analysis of Party Support in Britain, Germany and Switzerland', *European Societies*, 10:3, 329–55.

21 Dominik Geering and Silja Häusermann (2013) *Changing Party Electorates and Economic Realignment*. Zurich: Universität Zürich.

22 Gary W. Cox and Mathew D. McCubbins (1986) 'Electoral Politics as a Redistributive Game', *Journal of Politics*, 48, 370–89.
23 E.g. Paul Whiteley, Monica Poletti, Paul Webb and Tim Bale (2019) 'Oh Jeremy Corbyn! Why did Labour Party Membership Soar After the 2015 General Election', *The British Journal of Politics and International Relations*, 21:1, 80–98.
24 Mark Blyth (2002) *Great Transformations: Economic Ideas and Institutional Change in the Twentieth Century*. Cambridge: Cambridge University Press; Vivien A. Schmidt (2008) 'Discursive Institutionalism: The Explanatory Power of Ideas and Discourse', *Annual Review of Political Science*, 11:1, 303–26.

Bibliography

Ainsley, Claire (2018) *The New Working Class: How to Win Hearts, Minds and Votes*. Bristol: Policy Press.

Aitchison, Cara and Evans, Tom (2003) 'The Cultural Industries and a Model of Sustainable Regeneration: Manufacturing "Pop" in the Rhondda Valleys of South Wales', *Managing Leisure*, 8:3, 133–44.

Arendt, Hannah (1951) *The Origins of Totalitarianism*. New York: Harcourt Brace Jovanovich.

Arzheimer, Kai (2009) 'Contextual Factors and the Extreme Right Vote in Western Europe, 1980–2002', *American Journal of Political Science*, 53, 259–75.

Ashcraft, Richard (1972) 'Marx and Weber on Liberalism as Bourgeois Ideology', *Comparative Studies in Society and History*, 14:2, 130–68.

Australian Academy of Science. (2018) 'Why Evolution Isn't Perfect', Australian Academy of Science. Available at: www.science.org.au/curious/earth-environment/why-evolution-isnt-perfect. Accessed 17 May 2020.

Bailey, David, de Waele, Jean-Michel, Escalona, Fabien and Vieira, Mathieu (eds) (2016) *European Social Democracy During the Global Economic Crisis*. Manchester: Manchester University Press.

Bale, Tim (2016) *The Conservative Party: From Thatcher to Cameron*. Cambridge: Polity Press.

Bibliography

Bastani, Aaron (2019) *Fully Automated Luxury Communism*. New York: Verso Books.

Batson, C. Daniel (2011) *Altruism in Humans*. New York: Oxford University Press.

Beck, Ulrich (2012) 'Individualism', in G. Ritzer (ed.), *The Wiley-Blackwell Encyclopaedia of Globalization*. New Jersey: Blackwell.

Becker, Amy B. and Copeland, Lauren (2016) 'Networked Publics: How Connective Social Media Use Facilitates Political Consumerism Among LGBT Americans', *Journal of Information Technology & Politics*, 13:1, 22–36.

Bell, Torsten (2017) 'For Labour, It's All About What You Say', Resolution Foundation. Available at: www.resolutionfoundation.org/comment/for-labour-its-all-about-what-you-say/. Accessed 16 May 2020.

Berger, Peter L. and Luckmann, Thomas (1996) *The Social Construction of Reality: A Treatise in the Sociology of Knowledge*. New York: Garden City.

Bernstein, Eduard (1961) *Evolutionary Socialism: A Criticism and Affirmation*. New York: Schocken Books.

Berzins, Atis and Zvidrins, Peteris (2011) 'Depopulation in the Baltic States', *Lithuanian Journal of Statistics*, 50:1, 39–48.

Betz, Hans-Georg (2017) 'Nativism Across Time and Space', *Swiss Political Science Review*, 23:4, 335–53.

Biggs, Brian, King, Lawrence, Basu, Sanjay and Stuckler, David (2010) 'Is Wealthier Always Healthier? The Impact of National Income Level, Inequality, and Poverty on Public Health in Latin America', *Social Science & Medicine*, 71:2, 266–73.

Blyth, Mark (2002) *Great Transformations: Economic Ideas and Institutional Change in the Twentieth Century*. Cambridge: Cambridge University Press.

Bosse, Douglas A. and Phillips, Robert A. (2016) 'Agency Theory and Bounded Self-Interest', *Academy of Management Review*, 41:2, 276–97.

Bourdieu, Pierre (1984) *Distinction: A Social Critique of the Judgement of Taste*. Cambridge, MA: Harvard University Press.

Braithwaite, Valerie (2009) 'Attitudes to Tax Policy: Politics, Self-Interest and Social Values', Research Note 9, Centre for Tax System Integrity. Australian National University, Canberra.

Brennan, Jason (2016) *Against Democracy*. Princeton: Princeton University Press.

Brown, Stephanie L., Brown, R. Michael and Penner, Louis A. (eds) (2011) *Moving beyond Self-Interest: Perspectives from Evolutionary Biology, Neuroscience, and the Social Sciences*. Oxford: Oxford University Press.

Browne, James, O'Dea, Cormac and Phillips, David (2010) 'Personal Tax and Benefit Changes', Institute for Fiscal Studies. Available at: www.ifs.org.uk/budgets/budget2010/browne.pdf. Accessed 17 May 2020.

Burke, Edmund (1986) *Reflections on the Revolution in France (1790)*. Oxford: Oxford University Press.

Burns, Jonathan K., Tomita, Andrew and Kapadia, Amy S. (2014) 'Income Inequality and Schizophrenia: Increased Schizophrenia Incidence in Countries with High Levels of Income Inequality', *International Journal of Social Psychiatry*, 60:2, 185–96.

Cadwalladr, Carole (2016) 'Endless Lies Persuaded Ebbw Vale to Vote Leave', *Guardian*. Available at: www.theguardian.com/commentisfree/2016/jul/02/ebbw-vale-eu-vote-leave. Accessed 17 May 2020.

Cadwalladr, Carole (2019) 'Facebook's Role in Brexit and the Threat to Democracy', TED Talk. Available at: www.ted.com/talks/carole_cadwalladr_facebook_s_role_in_brexit_and_the_threat_to_democracy#t-161574. Accessed 17 May 2020.

Capoccia, Giovanni and Kelemen, R. Daniel (2007) 'The Study of Critical Junctures: Theory, Narrative, and Counterfactuals in Historical Institutionalism', *World Politics*, 59:3, 341–69.

Card, David, Dustmann, Christian and Preston, Ian (2012) 'Immigration, Wages, and Compositional Amenities', *Journal of European Economic Association*, 10:1, 78–119.

Carell, Severin (2014) 'Free Tuition in Scotland Benefits Wealthiest Students the Most – Study', *Guardian*. Available at: www.theguardian.com/education/2014/apr/29/free-tuition-scotland-benefits-wealthiest-students-most-study. Accessed 17 May 2020.

Bibliography

Carella, Leonardo and Ford, Robert (2020) 'The Status Stratification of Radical Right Support: Reconsidering the Occupational Profile of UKIP's Electorate'. Available at: www.drive.google.com/file/d/1gGxz5EQHaaxoVE5Jmgnn W1WnyzbD7WeD/view. Accessed 17 May 2020.

Carl, Noah (2019) 'Are Leave Voters Less Knowledgeable about the EU than Remain Voters?' Available at: www.ukandeu. ac.uk/are-leave-voters-less-knowledgeable-about-the-eu-than-remain-voters/. Accessed 19 January 2020.

Chan, Tak Wing, Henderson, Morag, Sironi, Maria and Kawalerowicz, Juta (2017) 'Understanding the Social and Cultural Bases of Brexit', Department of Quantitative Social Science, University College London.

Charalambous, Giorgos and Ioannou, Gregoris (2019) *Left Radicalism and Populism in Europe*. London: Routledge.

Chaudoin, Stephen, Milner, Helen V. and Pang, Xun (2015) 'International Systems and Domestic Politics: Linking Complex Interactions with Empirical Models in International Relations', *International Organization*, 69:2, 275–309.

Chomsky, Noam (2008) 'Humanitarian Imperialism: The New Doctrine of Imperial Right', *Monthly Review*, 60:4, 22–5.

Chong, Dennis and Druckman, James N. (2007) 'Framing Theory', *Annual Review of Political Science*, 10:1, 103–26.

Clegg, Stewart (2010) 'The State, Power, and Agency: Missing in Action in Institutional Theory?', *Journal of Management Inquiry*, 19:1, 4–13.

Cohen, Joshua (1997) 'Deliberation and Democratic Legitimacy', in J. Bohman and W. Rehg (eds), *Deliberative Democracy: Essays on Reason and Politics*. Cambridge, MA: Massachusetts Institute of Technology Press, 67–92.

Colomé, Jordi Pérez (2016) 'Podemos es el partido más votado entre las rentas medias y altas'. Available at: www.elpais. com/politica/2016/06/20/actualidad/1466448698_313220. html. Accessed 17 May 2020.

Colomy, Paul (1990) *Functionalist Sociology*. Cheltenham: Edward Elgar.

Costa, Rui and Machin, Stephen (2017) 'Real Wages and Living Standards in the UK'. Available from: http://cep.lse.ac.uk/ pubs/download/ea036.pdf. Accessed 19 January 2020.

Cox, Gary W. and McCubbins, Mathew D. (1986) 'Electoral Politics as a Redistributive Game', *Journal of Politics*, 48, 370–89.

Critchlow, Hannah (2019) *The Science of Fate: Why Your Future is More Predictable Than You Think*. London: Hachette Publishing.

Crosland, Anthony (2013) *The Future of Socialism*. New edition with foreword by Gordon Brown. London: Constable Publishing.

Dalton, Russell J. (2004) *Democratic Challenges, Democratic Choices: The Erosion of Political Support in Advanced Industrial Democracies*. Oxford: Oxford University Press.

Darley, John M. (2005) 'On the Unlikely Prospect of Reducing Crime Rates by Increasing the Severity of Prison Sentences', *Journal of Law and Policy*, 13:1, 189–208.

Dawkins, Richard (1976) *The Selfish Gene*. Oxford: Oxford University Press.

Davis, David Brion (1999) *The Problem of Slavery in The Age of Revolution, 1770–1823*. Oxford: Oxford University Press.

Davis-Blake, Alison and Uzzi, Brian (1993) 'Determinants of Employment Externalization: A Study of Temporary Workers and Independent Contractors', *Administrative Science Quarterly*, 38:2, 195–223.

De Koster, Willem, Achterberg, Peter and Van der Waal, Jeroen (2013) 'The New Right and the Welfare State: The Electoral Relevance of Welfare Chauvinism and Welfare Populism in the Netherlands', *International Political Science Review*, 34:1, 3–20.

De la Sablonniere, Roxane, Tougas, Francine, Taylor, Donald M., Crush, Jonathan, McDonald, David and Perenlei, Radchenko Onon (2015) 'Social Change in Mongolia and South Africa: The Impact of Relative Deprivation Trajectory and Group Status on Well-Being and Adjustment to Change', *Social Justice Research*, 28:1, 102–22.

Deneen, Patrick J. (2018) *Why Liberalism Failed*. Connecticut: Yale University Press.

De Waal, Frans B. M. (2008) 'Putting the Altruism Back into Altruism: The Evolution of Empathy', *Annual Review of Psychology*, 59:1, 279–99.

Dumont, Louis (1992) *Essays on Individualism: Modern Ideology in Anthropological Perspective*. Chicago: University of Chicago Press.

Dupré, Louis (1993) 'The Common Good and the Open Society', *The Review of Politics*, 55:4, 687–712.

Dustmann, Christian, Frattini, Tommaso and Preston, Ian P. (2012) 'The Effect of Immigration Along the Distribution of Wages', *Review of Economic Studies*, 80:1, 145–73.

Dustmann, Christian, Frattini, Tommaso and Rosso, Anna (2015) 'The Effect of Emigration from Poland on Polish Wages', *The Scandinavian Journal of Economics*, 117:2, 522–64.

Džuverovic, Nemanja (2013) 'Does More (or Less) Lead to Violence? Application of the Relative Deprivation Hypothesis on Economic Inequality-Induced Conflicts', *Croatian International Relations Review*, 19:68, 53–72.

Eastwood, Jonathan (2005) 'The Role of Ideas in Weber's Theory of Interests', *Critical Review*, 17:2, 89–100.

Eatwell, Roger and Goodwin, Matthew (2018) *National Populism: The Revolt against Liberal Democracy*. London: Pelican.

Eccleshall, Robert (2002) *English Conservatism since the Restoration: An Introduction and Anthology*. London: Routledge.

Eddo-Lodge, Reni (2018) *Why I'm No Longer Talking to White People about Race*. London: Bloomsbury.

Engelke, Matthew (2019) *How to Think Like an Anthropologist*. New Jersey: Princeton University Press.

Engels, Friedrich (1969) *The Principles of Communism*. Moscow: Progress Publishers.

Evans, Ceryn and Donnelly, Michael (2018) 'Deterred by Debt? Young People, Schools and the Escalating Cost of UK Higher Education', *Journal of Youth Studies*, 21:9, 1267–82.

Evans, Geoffrey and Tilley, James (2017) *The New Politics of Class: The Political Exclusion of the British Working Class*. Oxford: Oxford University Press.

Eyerman, Ron (1981) 'False Consciousness and Ideology in Marxist Theory', *Acta Sociologica*, 24:2, 43–56.

Ferrara, Alessandro (2018) 'Can Political Liberalism Help Us Rescue "the People" from Populism?', *Philosophy & Social Criticism*, 44:4, 463–77.

Fieldhouse, Edward, Green, Jane, Evans, Geoffrey, Mellon, Jonathan and Prosser, Christopher (2020) *British Election Study Internet Panel Wave 19*.

Follesdal, Andreas and Hix, Simon (2006) 'Why there is a Democratic Deficit in the EU: A Response to Majone and Moravcsik', *Journal of Common Market Studies*, 44:3, 533–62.

Ford, Robert and Lymperopoulou, Kitty (2017) 'Immigration', *British Social Attitudes 34*. Available at: www.bsa.natcen. ac.uk/media/39148/bsa34_immigration_final.pdf. Accessed 17 May 2020.

Foucault, Michel (1990) *The History of Sexuality: An Introduction, Volume I*. New York: Vintage.

Foucault, Michel (2012) *Discipline and Punish: The Birth of the Prison*. New York: Vintage.

Fraser, Nancy (2013) 'Feminism, Capitalism, and the Cunning of History', in *Fortunes of Feminism: From State-Managed Capitalism to Neoliberal Crisis*. London: Verso, 209–27.

Frattini, Tommaso (2014) 'Impact of Migration on UK Consumer Prices'. Available at: https://assets.publishing.service.gov. uk/government/uploads/system/uploads/attachment_data/ file/328006/Impact_of_migration_on_UK_consumer_prices_ _2014.pdf. Accessed 17 May 2020.

Freeden, Michael and Stears, Marc (2013) 'Liberalism', in M. Freeden, L. T. Sargent and M. Stears (eds), *The Oxford Handbook of Political Ideologies*. Oxford: Oxford University Press, 329–47.

Friedman, Milton (1970) 'Interview in The Donahue Show'. Available at: https://interviews.televisionacademy.com/ interviews/phil-donahue. Accessed 17 May 2020.

Friedman, Milton, Savage, Leonard J. and Becker, Gary S. (2007) *Milton Friedman on Economics: Selected Papers*. Chicago: University of Chicago Press.

Gabel, Matthew and Palmer, Harvey (1995) 'Understanding Variation in Public Support for European Integration', *European Journal of Political Research*, 27:1, 3–19.

Gamble, Andrew (2013) 'Economic Libertarianism', in M. Freeden, L. T. Sargent and M. Stears (eds), *The Oxford Handbook of Political Ideologies*. Oxford: Oxford University Press, 405–21.

Garrido, Hugo and Ley, Marta (2019) 'El voto de clase sigue existiendo: a menos renta, más votos para el PSOE'. Available at: www.elmundo.es/espana/2019/09/23/5d7bd6cafc6c83707e8b45b4.html. Accessed 17 May 2020.

Geering, Dominik and Häusermann, Silja (2013) *Changing Party Electorates and Economic Realignment*. Zurich: Universität Zürich.

Gest, Justin, Reny, Tyler and Mayer, Jeremy (2018) 'Roots of the Radical Right: Nostalgic Deprivation in the United States and Britain', *Comparative Political Studies*, 51:1, 1694–98.

Gingrich, Jane and Häusermann, Silja (2015) 'The Decline of the Working-Class Vote, the Reconfiguration of the Welfare Support Coalition and Consequences for the Welfare State', *Journal of European Social Policy*, 25:3, 50–75.

Golder, Matt (2003) 'Explaining Variation in the Success of Extreme Right Parties in Western Europe', *Comparative Political Studies*, 36:4, 432–66.

Goodhart, David (2017) *The Road to Somewhere: The Populist Revolt and the Future of Politics*. London: C. Hurst & Co.

Goodin, Robert E. and Le Grand, Julian (2018) *Not Only the Poor: The Middle Classes and the Welfare State*. London: Routledge.

Goodwin, Matthew and Heath, Oliver (2016) 'The 2016 Referendum, Brexit and the Left Behind: An Aggregate-Level Analysis of the Result', *The Political Quarterly*, 87:3, 323–32.

Goren, Paul (2005) 'Party Identification and Core Political Values', *American Journal of Political Science*, 49:4, 881–96.

Graff, Cristina C. Santamaria (2017) '"Build That Wall!"': Manufacturing the Enemy, Yet Again', *International Journal of Qualitative Studies in Education*, 30:10, 999–1005.

Gusfield, Joseph R. (1986) *Symbolic Crusade: Status Politics and the American Temperance Movement*. Chicago: University of Illinois Press.

Haidt, Jonathan (2012) *The Righteous Mind: Why Good People are Divided by Politics and Religion*. New York: Random House.

Hainmueller, Jens and Hiscox, Michael J. (2010) 'Attitudes toward Highly Skilled and Low-Skilled Immigration: Evidence from a Survey Experiment', *American Political Science Review*, 104:1, 61–84.

Hainmueller, Jens and Hopkins, Daniel J. (2014) 'Public Attitudes toward Immigration', *Annual Review of Political Science*, 17:1, 225–49.

Hakim, Catherine (2000) *Work-Lifestyle Choices in the 21st Century: Preference Theory*. Oxford: Oxford University Press.

Han, Byung-chul (2015) 'Why Revolution is no Longer Possible', Open Democracy. Available at: www.opendemocracy.net/en/transformation/why-revolution-is-no-longer-possible/. Accessed 17 May 2020.

Handley, John (2020) 'Starmer is More Popular than Corbyn among Both the Self-Identifying Working Class and People in Lower NS-SEC Classes'. Available at: https://twitter.com/jwhandley17/status/1250763886938095618. Accessed 17 May 2020.

Harris, Jose (2017) 'Principles, Markets and National Interest in Conservative Approaches to Social Policy', in C. Berthezène and J.-C. Vinel (eds), *Postwar Conservatism: A Transnational Investigation*. London: Palgrave Macmillan, 95–118.

Harsanyi, David (2014) *The People Have Spoken (and They Are Wrong): The Case Against Democracy*. Washington, DC: Regnery.

Hart, Kim (2018) 'Exclusive Poll: Only Half of Americans Have Faith in Democracy', *Axios*. Available at: www.axios.com/poll-americans-faith-in-democracy-2e94a938-4365-4e80-9fb6-d9743d817710.html. Accessed 17 May 2020.

Hasell, Ariel and Weeks, Brian E. (2016) 'Partisan Provocation: The Role of Partisan News Use and Emotional Responses in Political Information Sharing in Social Media', *Human Communication Research*, 42:4, 641–61.

Hastings, Annette and Matthews, Peter (2011) 'Sharp Elbows: Do the Middle-Classes Have Advantages in Public Service Provision and If So How?' Glasgow: University of Glasgow.

Hayek, Friedrich (2014) *The Road to Serfdom: Text and Documents: The Definitive Edition*. London: Routledge.

Hayton, Richard (2018) 'British Conservatism after the Vote for Brexit: The Ideological Legacy of David Cameron', *The British Journal of Politics and International Relations*, 20:1, 223–38.

Heath, Oliver and Goodwin, Matthew (2019) 'Low-Income Voters in UK General Elections, 1987 – 2017', Joseph

Rowntree Foundation. Available at: www.jrf.org.uk/ report/low-income-voters-uk-general-elections-1987-2017. Accessed 17 May 2020.

Hobolt, Sara B. (2016) 'The Brexit Vote: A Divided Nation, a Divided Continent', *Journal of European Public Policy*, 23:9, 1259–77.

Hochschild, Arlie Russell (2018) *Strangers in their Own Land: Anger and Mourning on the American Right*. New York: The New Press.

Hoffarth, Mark R. and Jost, John T. (2017) 'When Ideology Contradicts Self-Interest: Conservative Opposition to Same-Sex Marriage among Sexual Minorities – a Commentary on Pinsof and Haselton', *Psychological Science*, 28:10, 1521–24.

Hoolachan, Jennifer, McKee, Kim, Moore, Tom and Soaita, Adriana Mihael (2017) '"Generation Rent" and the Ability to "Settle Down": Economic and Geographical Variation in Young People's Housing Transitions', *Journal of Youth Studies*, 20:1, 63–78.

Huskinson, Tom, Hobden, Sylvie, Oliver, Dominic, Keyes, Jennifer, Littlewood, Mandy, Pye, Julia and Tipping, Sarah (2016) 'Childcare and Early Years Survey of Parents 2014–2015', The UK Government Publication – Department for Education. Available at: www.gov.uk/government/statistics/ childcare-and-early-years-survey-of-parents-2014-to-2015. Accessed 17 May 2020.

Inequality Briefing. (2015) 'Briefing 61: Regional Inequality in the UK is the Worst in Western Europe'. Available at: www.inequalitybriefing.org/brief/briefing-61-regional-inequality-in-the-uk-is-the-worst-in-western-europe. Accessed 17 May 2020.

Inequality in Transport. (2018) 'What it Costs to Travel'. Available at: www.inequalityintransport.org.uk/exploring-transport-inequality/what-it-costs-travel. Accessed 17 May 2020.

Inglehart, Ronald (1977) *The Silent Revolution: Changing Values and Political Styles among Western Publics*. Princeton: Princeton University Press.

Institute for Fiscal Studies. (2017) 'General Election Analysis 2017'. Available at: www.ifs.org.uk/uploads/Presentations/Rob%20 Joyce%2C%202017%20General%20Election%2C%20mani-festo%20analysis.pdf. Accessed 17 May 2020.

Institute for Fiscal Studies. (2019) 'Party Manifestoes'. Available at: www.ifs.org.uk/election/2019/manifestos. Accessed 17 May 2020.

Jackman, Robert W. and Volpert, Karin (1996) 'Conditions Favouring Parties of the Extreme Right in Western Europe', *British Journal of Political Science*, 26:1, 501–21.

Jackson, Ben (2013) 'Social Democracy', in M. Freeden, L. T. Sargent and M. Stears (eds), *The Oxford Handbook of Political Ideologies*. Oxford: Oxford University Press, 348–63.

Jennings, Will, Stoker, Gerry and Warren, Ian (2019) 'Cities and Towns: The Geography of Discontent', in *Brexit and Public Opinion 2019: UK in a Changing Europe*. Available at: www. ukandeu.ac.uk/wp-content/uploads/2019/01/Public-opinion-2019.pdf. Accessed 17 May 2020.

Jervis, Robert (1999) 'Realism, Neoliberalism, and Cooperation: Understanding the Debate', *International Security*, 24:1, 42–63.

Johnson, Dominic D. P. and Fowler, James H. (2011) 'The Evolution of Overconfidence', *Nature*, 477:1, 317–20.

Jones, Owen (2012) 'The Tories Do Have Policies: They Just Don't Want You to Know What They Are', *Guardian*. Available at: www.theguardian.com/commentisfree/2019/ dec/05/the-tories-do-have-policies-they-just-dont-want-you-to-know-what-they-are. Accessed 17 May 2020.

Jost, John T., Fitzsimons, Gráinne and Kay, Aaron C. (2004) 'The Ideological Animal: A System Justification View', in J. Greenberg, S. L. Koole and T. A. Pyszczynski (eds), *Handbook of Experimental Existential Psychology*. New York: Guilford Press, 263–82.

Joyce, Robert, Pope, Thomas and Roantree, Barra (2019) 'The Characteristics and Incomes of the Top 1%', Institute for Fiscal Studies. Available at: www.ifs.org.uk/publications/ 14303. Accessed 17 May 2020.

Judt, Tony (2006) *Postwar: A History of Europe since 1945*. New York: Penguin.

Kamm, Oliver (2019) 'Labour's WASPI Pledge is a Regressive Outrage', CAPX. Available at: www.capx.co/labours-waspi-pledge-is-a-regressive-outrage/. Accessed 17 May 2020.

Keller, Reiner (2011) 'The Sociology of Knowledge Approach to Discourse (SKAD)', *Human Studies*, 34:1, 43–45.

Kelley, Nancy, Warhurst, Christopher and Wishart, Robert (2018) 'Work and Welfare: The Changing Face of the UK Labour Market', in D. Phillips, J. Curtice, M. Phillips and J. Perry (eds), *British Social Attitudes: The 35th Report*. London: The National Centre for Social Research.

Kenny, Michael (1995) *The First New Left*. London: Lawrence & Wishart.

Kiely, Ray (2005) 'Capitalist Expansion and the Imperialism–Globalization Debate: Contemporary Marxist Explanations', *Journal of International Relations and Development*, 8:1, 27–57.

Kitschelt, Herbert (1994) *The Transformation of European Social Democracy*. Cambridge: Cambridge University Press.

Koeppel, Maria D. H., Rhineberger-Dunn, Gayle M. and Mack, Kristen Y. (2015) 'Cross-National Homicide: A Review of the Current Literature', *International Journal of Comparative and Applied Criminal Justice*, 39:1, 47–85.

Kołakowski, Leszek (1982) 'What is Living (and what is Dead) in the Social-Democratic Idea?', *Encounter*, 58, 11–17.

Kollman, Kelly (2014) 'Deploying Europe: The Creation of Discursive Imperatives for Same-Sex Unions', in D. Paternotte and P. Ayoub (eds), *LGBT Activism and the Making of Europe*. London: Palgrave Macmillan, 97–118.

Kologlugil, Serhat (2015) 'Digitizing Karl Marx: The New Political Economy of General Intellect and Immaterial Labour', *Rethinking Marxism*, 27:1, 123–37.

Kriesi, Hanspeter, Grande, Edgar, Lachat, Romain, Dolezal, Martin, Bornschier, Simon and Frey, Timotheos (2008) *West European Politics in the Age of Globalization*. Cambridge: Cambridge University Press.

Lakner, Christoph and Milanovic, Branko (2016) 'Global Income Distribution: From the Fall of the Berlin Wall to the Great Recession', *World Bank Economic Review*, 30:2, 203–32.

Lavelle, Ashley (2016) *The Death of Social Democracy: Political Consequences in the 21st Century*. London: Routledge.

Lee, Neil, Morris, Katy and Kemeny, Thomas (2018) 'Immobility and the Brexit Vote', *Cambridge Journal of Regions, Economy and Society*, 11:1, 143–63.

Lenin, Vladimir (2013) *What is to be Done?* Beijing: Foreign Languages Press.

Lewis, Orion A. and Steinmo, Sven (2012) 'How Institutions Evolve: Evolutionary Theory and Institutional Change', *Polity*, 44:3, 314–39.

Lilla, Mark (2018) *The Once and Future Liberal: After Identity Politics*. Oxford: Oxford University Press.

Lin, Nan (2001) *Social Capital: A Theory of Social Structure and Action*. Cambridge: Cambridge University Press.

Lindbeck, Assar and Weibull, Jörgen W. (1987) 'Balanced-Budget Redistribution as the Outcome of Political Competition', *Public Choice*, 52:3, 273–97.

Lipset, Seymour Martin (1959) 'Democracy and Working-Class Authoritarianism', *American Sociological Review*, 24:4, 482–97.

Lipset, Seymour Martin (1981) *Political Man: The Social Bases of Politics*. Baltimore: Johns Hopkins University Press.

Lipsey, David (2016) 'Liberal Interventionism', *The Political Quarterly*, 87:3, 415–23.

Loxbo, Karl, Hinnfors, Jonas, Hagevi, Magnus, Blombäck, Sofie and Demker, Marie (2019) 'The Decline of Western European Social Democracy: Exploring the Transformed Link between Welfare State Generosity and the Electoral Strength of Social Democratic Parties, 1975–2014', *Party Politics*. Online First. Available at: https://journals.sagepub.com/doi/full/10.1177/1354068819861339. Accessed 19 July 2020.

Lubbers, Marcel, Gijsberts, Mérove and Scheepers, Peer (2002) 'Extreme Right-Wing Voting in Western Europe', *European Journal of Political Research*, 4:1, 345–78.

Lukes, Steven (1982) 'Can a Marxist Believe in Human Rights?', *Praxis International*, 1:4, 334–45.

Bibliography

McGuiness, Feargal and Harari, Daniel (2019) 'Income Inequality in the UK', UK Government Report. Available at: www.researchbriefings.files.parliament.uk/documents/CBP-7484/CBP-7484.pdf. Accessed 17 May 2020.

MacKay, Brad (2016) 'Does Business Really Support "Remain" in the EU Referendum Debate?'. Business Views on the EU Referendum. Media Briefing, Centre on Constitutional Change, University of St Andrews, 20. Available at: www.centreonconstitutionalchange.ac.uk/sites/default/files/migrated/papers/Business%20Surveys%20EU%20Referendum_210616.pdf. Accessed 9 February 2020.

Malka, Ariel, Lelkes, Yphtach and Soto, Christopher J. (2017) 'Are Cultural and Economic Conservatism Positively Correlated? A Large-Scale Cross-National Test', *British Journal of Political Science*, 49:3, 1–25.

Mannheim, Karl (1960) *Ideology and Utopia: An Introduction to the Sociology of Knowledge*. London: Routledge.

Maraña, Jesus (2017) *Al Fondo a la Izquierda*. Barcelona: Planeta.

Marglin, Stephen A. and Schor, Juliet B. (1991) *The Golden Age of Capitalism: Reinterpreting the Post War Experience*. Oxford: Oxford University Press.

Marmot, Michael and Bobak, Martin (2000) 'International Comparators and Poverty and Health in Europe', *British Medical Journal*, 321:1, 11–24.

Martin, Nicole, Sobolewska, Maria and Begum, Neema (2019) 'Left Out of the Left Behind: Ethnic Minority Support for Brexit', Social Science Research Network.

Mason, Paul (2016) 'Brexit is a Fake Revolt: Working Class Culture is Being Hijacked to Help the Elite', *Guardian*. Available at: www.theguardian.com/commentisfree/2016/jun/20/brexit-fake-revolt-eu-working-class-culture-hijacked-help-elite. Accessed 17 May 2020.

Mastromatteo, Giuseppe and Russo, Francesca Flaviano (2017) 'Inequality and Charity', *World Development*, 96:1, 136–44.

Masullo-Chen, Gina and Lu, Shuning (2017) 'Online Political Discourse: Exploring Differences in Effects of Civil and Uncivil Disagreement in News Website Comments', *Journal of Broadcasting & Electronic Media*, 61:1, 108–25.

Bibliography

Mearsheimer, John J. (2010) 'Why is Europe Peaceful Today?', *European Political Science*, 9:3, 387–97.

Mellon, Jonathan and Prosser, Christopher (2017) 'Authoritarianism, Social Structure and Economic Policy Preferences', Social Science Research Network.

Merkel, Wolfgang (1991) 'After the Golden Age: Is Social Democracy Doomed to Decline?', in C. Lemke and G. Marks (eds), *The Crisis of Socialism in Europe*. Durham, NC: Duke University Press.

Meyer, Thomas and Hinchman, Lewis (2007) *The Theory of Social Democracy*. Cambridge: Polity.

Milanovic, Branko (2016) *Global Inequality: A New Approach for the Age of Globalization*. Cambridge, MA: Harvard University Press.

Miller, Arthur (2003) *The Crucible*. London: Penguin.

Moorby, Martin (2018) 'Who is this Man Who is Distinct from this Citizen: Revisiting Marx's Critique of Liberal Rights', *Journal of Cultural Studies of Association*, 7:1.

Mouffe, Chantal (2018) *For a Left Populism*. London: Verso Books.

Mounk, Yascha (2018) *The People vs. Democracy: Why Our Freedom is in Danger and How to Save it*. Cambridge, MA: Harvard University Press.

Mudde, Cas and Rovira Kaltwasser, Cristóbal (2018) 'Studying Populism in Comparative Perspective: Reflections on the Contemporary and Future Research Agenda', *Comparative Political Studies*, 51:13, 1667–93.

Müller, Jan-Werner. (2016) *What is Populism?* Philadelphia: University of Pennsylvania Press.

Murray, Christopher and Chambers, Ray (2015) 'Keeping Score: Fostering Accountability for Children's Lives', *The Lancet*, 386:98, 5–10.

Naczelna Izba Pielęgniarek i Położnych. (2018) 'Raport Naczelnej Rady Pielęgniarek i Położnych: zabezpieczenie społeczeństwa polskiego w świadczenia pielęgniarek i położnych'. Available at: www.nipip.pl/wp-content/uploads/2017/03/Raport_druk_2017.pdf. Accessed 9 February 2020.

Nickell, Stephen and Saleheen, Jumana (2015) 'The Impact of Immigration on Occupational Wages: Evidence from Britain', Bank of England Working Paper 574.

Norris, Pippa and Inglehart, Ronald (2019) *Cultural Backlash: Trump, Brexit, and Authoritarian Populism.* Cambridge: Cambridge University Press.

Nyhan, Brendan and Reifler, Jason (2010) 'When Corrections Fail: The Persistence of Political Misperceptions', *Political Behaviour*, 32:2, 303–30.

Oesch, Daniel (2008) 'The Changing Shape of Class Voting: An Individual-Level Analysis of Party Support in Britain, Germany and Switzerland', *European Societies*, 10:3, 329–55.

Oesch, Daniel (2008) 'Explaining Workers' Support for Right-Wing Populist Parties in Western Europe: Evidence from Austria, Belgium, France, Norway, and Switzerland'. *International Political Science Review*, 29:3, 349–73.

Osberg, Lars and Smeeding, Timothy (2004) 'Fair Inequality? An International Comparison of Attitudes to Pay Differentials', Dalhousie University. Available at: www. wwwcpr. maxwell.syr.edu/faculty/smeeding/selectedpapers/ Economicaversion27October2004.pdf. Accessed 17 May 2020.

Osborne, Danny and Sibley, Chris G. (2015) 'Opposing Paths to Ideology: Group-Based Relative Deprivation Predicts Conservatism through Warmth toward Ingroup and Outgroup Members', *Social Justice Research*, 28:1, 27–51.

O'Sullivan, Noel (2013) 'Conservatism', in M. Freeden, L. T. Sargent and M. Stears (eds), *The Oxford Handbook of Political Ideologies*. Oxford: Oxford University Press, 293–311.

Oxford Economics. (2018) 'The Fiscal Impact of Immigration on the UK'. Available at: www.oxfordeconomics.com/recent-releases/8747673d-3b26-439b-9693-0e250df6dbba. Accessed 17 May 2020.

Pabst, Adrian (2019) *The Demons of Liberal Democracy.* Cambridge: Polity Press.

Panayotakis, Costas (2011) *Remaking Scarcity: From Capitalist Inefficiency to Economic Democracy.* London: Pluto.

Parry, Geraint, Moyser, George and Day, Neil (1992) *Political Participation and Democracy in Britain.* Cambridge: Cambridge University Press.

Payne, Geoff and Williams, Malcolm (2005) 'Generalization in Qualitative Research', *Sociology*, 39:2, 295–314.

Peters, B. Guy (2019) *Institutional Theory in Political Science: The New Institutionalism*. Cheltenham: Edward Elgar.

Pickett, Kate E. and Wilkinson, Richard G. (2015) 'Income Inequality and Health: A Causal Review', *Social Science & Medicine*, 128:2, 316–26.

Pierson, Paul (2000) 'Increasing Returns, Path Dependence, and the Study of Politics', *American Political Science Review*, 94:2, 251–67.

Piketty, Thomas (2014) *Capital in the Twenty-First Century*. Cambridge, MA: Harvard University Press.

Polanyi, Karl (1994) *The Great Transformation*. New York: Farrar & Rinehart.

Poletti, Monica, Bale, Tim and Webb, Paul (2016) 'Explaining the Pro-Corbyn Surge in Labour's Membership', London School of Economics: European Politics and Policy. Available at: https://blogs.lse.ac.uk/politicsandpolicy/explaining-the-pro-corbyn-surge-in-labours-membership/. Accessed 16 May 2020.

Pontusson, Jonas (1995) 'Explaining the Decline of European Social Democracy: The Role of Structural Economic Change', *World Politics*, 47:4, 502–33.

Popper, Karl Raimund (1945) *The Open Society and its Enemies*. London: Routledge.

Powell, Robert (2003) 'Nuclear Deterrence Theory, Nuclear Proliferation, and National Missile Defence', *International Security*, 27:4, 86–91.

Prosser, Thomas (2016) 'Economic Union without Social Union: The Strange Case of the European Social Dialogue', *Journal of European Social Policy*, 26:5, 460–72.

Prosser, Thomas (2017) 'Explaining Implementation through Varieties of Capitalism Theory: The Case of the Telework and Work-Related Stress Agreements', *Journal of Common Market Studies*, 55:4, 889–908.

Prosser, Thomas (2018) *European Labour Movements in Crisis: From Indecision to Indifference*. Manchester: Manchester University Press.

Prosser, Thomas (2020) 'Who are the New Conservative Voters and What Socio-Economic Policies Do They Want? Some Pre-Budget Analysis', blog entry. Available at: https://thomasjprosser.wordpress.com/2020/03/10/who-are-the-new-conservative-voters-and-what-socio-economic-policies-do-they-want-some-pre-budget-analysis/. Accessed 17 May 2020.

Prosser, Thomas (2020) 'Budget 2020: Why the Conservatives are Placing More Emphasis on Redistribution', LSE British Politics and Policy. Available at: https://blogs.lse.ac.uk/politicsandpolicy/budget-2020-redistribution/. Accessed 17 May 2020.

Prosser, Thomas and Giorgadze, Giga (2018) 'Towards a Theory of Illiberal Dualisation? Conceptualising New Employment and Social Policy Divisions in Poland and the United Kingdom', *Transfer: European Review of Labour and Research*, 24:2, 151–62.

Putnam, Robert D. (2000) *Bowling Alone: The Collapse and Revival of American Community*. New York: Simon & Schuster.

Radelet, Michael and Akers, Ronald L. (1996) 'Deterrence and the Death Penalty: The Views of the Experts', *The Journal of Criminal Law and Criminology*, 87:1, 1–16.

Rees, Teresa (1998) *Mainstreaming Equality in the European Union: Education, Training and Labour Market Policies*. London: Routledge.

Rho, Sungmin and Tomz, Michael (2017) 'Why Don't Trade Preferences Reflect Economic Self-Interest?', *International Organization*, 71:1, 85–108.

Roberts, Adrienne (2012) 'Financial Crisis, Financial Firms ... and Financial Feminism? The Rise of "Transnational Business Feminism" and the Necessity of Marxist-Feminist IPE', *Socialist Studies*, 8:2, 85–108.

Rooduijn, Matthijs and Burgoon, Brian (2018) 'The Paradox of Wellbeing: Do Unfavourable Socioeconomic and Sociocultural Contexts Deepen or Dampen Radical Left and Right Voting among the Less Well-Off?', *Comparative Political Studies*, 51:13, 1720–53.

Ruhs, Martin and Vargas-Silva, Carlos (2017) 'Briefing: The Labour Market Effects of Immigration'. The Migration Observatory. Available at: http://migrationobservatory.ox.ac.uk/wp-content/uploads/2016/04/Briefing-Labour_Market_Effects_Immigration.pdf. Accessed 17 May 2020.

Runciman, David (2018) *How Democracy Ends*. London: Profile Books.

Runciman, Walter Garrison (1996) *Relative Deprivation and Social Justice: A Study of Attitudes to Social Inequality in Twentieth-Century England* (Vol. 13). Berkeley: University of California Press.

Rushton, J. Philippe, Russell, Robin J. H. and Wells, Pamela (1984) 'Genetic Similarity Theory: Beyond Kin Selection', *Behaviour Genetics*, 14:3, 179–93.

Ryan, Frances (2016) 'Martin's Already Lost Almost Everything: He Voted Leave to Spread the Pain', *Guardian*. Available at: www.theguardian.com/commentisfree/2016/jun/30/martin-nothing-lose-vote-leave-unemployed-benefits-sanctioned. Accessed 17 May 2020.

Rydgren, Jens (2003) 'Meso-Level Reasons for Racism and Xenophobia: Some Converging and Diverging Effects of Radical Right Populism in France and Sweden', *European Journal of Social Theory*, 6:1, 45–68.

Rydgren, Jens (2013) *Class Politics and the Radical Right*. London: Routledge.

Rydgren, Jens and Ruth, Patrick (2013) 'Contextual Explanations of Radical Right-Wing Support in Sweden: Socioeconomic Marginalization, Group Threat, and the Halo Effect', *Ethnic and Racial Studies*, 36:4, 711–28.

Sandler, Joseph and Perlow, Meir (2018) 'Internalization and Externalization', in J. Sandler (ed.), *Projection, Identification, Projective Identification*. London: Routledge, 1–11.

Schall, Carly Elizabeth (2016) *The Rise and Fall of the Miraculous Welfare Machine: Immigration and Social Democracy in Twentieth-Century Sweden*. New York: Cornell University Press.

Scheidel, Walter (2018) *The Great Leveler: Violence and the History of Inequality from the Stone Age to the Twenty-First Century*. Princeton: Princeton University Press.

Schmidt, Vivien A. (2008) 'Discursive Institutionalism: The Explanatory Power of Ideas and Discourse', *Annual Review of Political Science*, 11:1, 303–26.

Schmidt, Vivien A. (2014) 'Speaking to the Markets or to the People? A Discursive Institutionalist Analysis of the EU's Sovereign Debt Crisis', *The British Journal of Politics and International Relations*, 16:1, 188–209.

Schrank, Phillip Gary (2017) 'The Rise of Populism and the Future of NATO', *Global Politics Review*, 3:2, 53–62.

Seidel, Markus (2011) 'Relativism or Relationism? A Mannheimian Interpretation of Fleck's Claims about Relativism', *Journal for General Philosophy of Science*, 42:2, 219–40.

Shiller, Robert J., Boycko, Maxim and Korobov, Vladimir (1990) 'Popular Attitudes towards Free Markets: The Soviet Union and the United States Compared', *American Economic Review*, 8:3, 385–400.

Siedentop, Larry (2014) *Inventing the Individual*. Cambridge, MA: Harvard University Press.

Simmons, Rob E. and Altwegg, Res (2010) 'Necks-for-Sex or Competing Browsers? A Critique of Ideas on the Evolution of Giraffe', *Journal of Zoology*, 282:1, 6–12.

Slaughter, Anne-Marie (2004) *A New World Order*. Princeton: Princeton University Press.

Smith, Adam (2010) *The Wealth of Nations: An Inquiry into the Nature and Causes of the Wealth of Nations*. Petersfield: Harriman House Limited.

Smith, Matthew (2016) 'Election Data Survey Results: 2016 Labour Leadership Election', *Politics and Current Affairs*. Available at: www.d25d2506sfb94s.cloudfront.net/cumulus_uploads/document/a8ttjtolgq/ElectionDataResults_160923_FinalCall.pdf. Accessed 17 May 2020.

Spier, Tim (2010) *Modernisierungsverlierer? Die Wählerschaft rechtspopulistischer Parteien in Westeuropa*. Wiesbaden: VS Verlag für Sozialwissenschaften.

Staiger, Uta, Pagel, Christina and Cooper, Christabel (2019) 'With No-Deal Now Leavers' Preferred Brexit Outcome, Ruling It Out Could Create Problems for the Tories'. Available at:

Bibliography

www.huffingtonpost.co.uk/entry/no-deal-leavers_uk_
5ca902dae4b0a00f6d408928. Accessed 17 May 2020.

Stein, Jeff (2016) 'Bernie Sanders's Base isn't the Working Class.
It's Young People', *Vox*. Available at: www.vox.com/2016/5/
19/11649054/bernie-sanders-working-class-base. Accessed 17
May 2020.

Stevens, Martin, Cuthill, Innes C., Windsor, Amy M. M. and
Walker, Hannah J. (2006) 'Disruptive Contrast in Animal
Camouflage', *Proceedings of the Royal Society B: Biological
Sciences*, 273:1600, 2433–8.

Streeck, Wolfgang (1998) 'The Internationalization of Industrial
Relations in Europe: Prospects and Problems', *Politics &
Society*, 26:4, 429–59.

Streeck, Wolfgang (2005) 'Rejoinder: On Terminology,
Functionalism (Historical) Institutionalism and Liberalization',
Socio-Economic Review, 3:3, 577–87.

Streeck, Wolfgang (2016) *How Will Capitalism End? Essays on a
Failing System*. New York: Verso Books.

Surridge, Paula (2016) 'Education and Liberalism: Pursuing the
Link', *Oxford Review of Education*, 42:2, 146–64.

Swank, Duane and Betz, Hans-Georg (2003) 'Globalization, the
Welfare State and Right-Wing Populism in Western Europe',
Socio-Economic Review, 1:2, 215–45.

Sykes, Alan (1997) *The Rise and Fall of British Liberalism: 1776–
1988*. London: Routledge.

Taylor, Eleanor Attar and Scott, Jacqueline (2018) 'Gender: New
Consensus or Continuing Battleground?', in D. Phillips,
J. Curtice, M. Phillips and J. Perry (eds), *British Social
Attitudes: The 35th Report*. London: The National Centre for
Social Research, 56–85.

Thelen, Kathleen (1999) 'Historical Institutionalism in
Comparative Politics', *Annual Review of Political Science*,
2:1, 369–404.

Timmins, Nicholas (2001) *The Five Giants: A Biography of the
Welfare State*. New York: HarperCollins.

Trottier, Daniel and Fuchs, Christian (2014) *Social Media,
Politics and the State: Protests, Revolutions, Riots, Crime*

and Policing in the Age of Facebook, Twitter and YouTube. London: Routledge.

Turner, Bryan S. (1998) 'Individualism, Capitalism and the Dominant Culture: A Note on the Debate', *The Australian and New Zealand Journal of Sociology*, 24:1, 47–64.

Van den Bos, Kees, Van Veldhuizen, Tanja S. and Au, Al K. C. (2015) 'Counter Cross-Cultural Priming and Relative Deprivation: The Role of Individualism–Collectivism', *Social Justice Research*, 28:1, 52–75.

Van de Werfhorst, Herman G. and de Graaf, Nan Dirk (2004) 'The Sources of Political Orientations in Post-Industrial Society: Social Class and Education Revisited', *The British Journal of Sociology*, 55:2, 211–35.

Van Evera, Stephen (1998) 'Offense, Defense, and the Causes of War', *International Security*, 22:4, 5–43.

Van Reybrouck, David (2016) *Against Elections: The Case for Democracy*. London: Bodley Head.

Varshney, Ashutosh (2003) 'Nationalism, Ethnic Conflict, and Rationality', *Perspectives on Politics*, 1:1, 85–99.

Vincent, Andrew (1998) 'New Ideologies for Old?', *The Political Quarterly*, 69:1, 48–58.

Vobruba, Georg (1983) *Politik mit dem Wohlfahrtsstaat.* Frankfurt: Suhrkamp.

Wall, Irwin M. (1977) 'The French Communists and the Algerian War', *Journal of Contemporary History*, 12:3, 521–43.

Wallace, Elaine, Buil, Isabel and De Chernatony, Leslie (2018) ' "Consuming Good" on Social Media: What Can Conspicuous Virtue Signalling on Facebook Tell Us About Prosocial and Unethical Intentions?', *Journal of Business Ethics*, 162:1, 557–92.

Walsh, David, McCartney, Gerry, McCullough, Sarah, van der Pol, Marjon, Buchanan, Duncan and Jones, Russell (2015) 'Comparing Levels of Social Capital in Three Northern Post-Industrial UK Cities', *Public Health*, 129:6, 629–38.

Wąsowski, Michał (2014) 'Tusk przeprasza za to, że chciał obniżać podatki. Kiedyś mówił: "Kieszeń podatnika jest nadmiernie obciążona"'. Available at: www.natemat.pl/ 100997,tusk-kiedys-chcial-obnizac-podatki. Accessed 17 May 2020.

Bibliography

Webb, Paul and Bale, Tim (2014) 'Why Do Tories Defect to UKIP? Conservative Party Members and the Temptations of the Populist Radical Right', *Political Studies*, 62:4, 961–70.

Weber, Max, Gerth, Hans Heinrich and Mills, C. Wright (1946) *Max Weber: Essays in Sociology*. Oxford: Oxford University Press.

Weiss, Thomas G., Thakur, Ramesh and Ruggie, John Gerard (2010) *Global Governance and the UN: An Unfinished Journey*. Indiana: Indiana University Press.

Whiteley, Paul, Clarke, Harold D., Sanders, David and Stewart, Marianne (2016) 'Why Do Voters Lose Trust in Governments? Public Perceptions of Government Honesty and Trustworthiness in Britain 2000–2013', *The British Journal of Politics and International Relations*, 18:1, 234–54.

Whiteley, Paul, Poletti, Monica, Webb, Paul and Bale, Tim (2019) 'Oh Jeremy Corbyn! Why did Labour Party Membership Soar After the 2015 General Election', *The British Journal of Politics and International Relations*, 21:1, 80–98.

Wilson, Glenn D. (1973) *The Psychology of Conservatism*. London: Academic Press.

Wistrich, Robert S. (1990) 'Left-Wing Anti-Zionism in Western Societies', in R. S. Wistrich (ed.), *Anti-Zionism and Antisemitism in the Contemporary World*. London: Palgrave Macmillan, 46–52.

Woodburn, James (1982) 'Egalitarian Societies', *Man New Series*, 17:3, 431–51.

Woodwell, Douglas (2007) *Nationalism in International Relations: Norms, Foreign Policy, and Enmity*. New York: Springer.

Yilmaz, Ferruh (2012) 'Right-Wing Hegemony and Immigration: How the Populist Far-Right Achieved Hegemony through the Immigration Debate in Europe', *Current Sociology*, 60:3, 368–81.

YouGov. (2016) 'Election Data Survey Results: 2016 Labour Leadership Election', *Politics and Current Affairs*. Available at: www.d25d2506sfb94s.cloudfront.net/cumulus_uploads/document/a8ttjtolgq/ElectionDataResults_160923_FinalCall.pdf. Accessed 17 May 2020.

YouGov. (2018) 'Survey Results'. Available at: www. d 2 5 d 2 5 0 6 s f b 9 4 s . c l o u d f r o n t . n e t / c u m u l u s _ up-loads/document/iopahgu564/InternalResults_180205_ Feminism_Suffragettes_w.pdf. Accessed 17 May 2020.

Younge, Gary (2010) 'I Hate Tories. And Yes, It's Tribal', *Guardian*. Available at: www.theguardian.com/ commentisfree/2010/may/04/why-i-hate-tories-david-cameron. Accessed 17 May 2020.

Younge, Gary (2019) 'Trump's a Racist Conman – and that's the Brand America Bought', *Guardian*. Available at: www. theguardian.com/commentisfree/2019/feb/28/donald-trump-michael-cohen-racist-conman-america. Accessed 17 May 2020.

Index

Note: Page numbers for figures and tables appear in *italics*.

500+ child benefit policy 57

abuse 125
addiction 40
affiliation 95
Africa 113
Against Democracy 99
Against Elections 99
age 9, 22, 68, 108, 124
  see also young middle
    classes
Alternative for Germany 55
altruism 17–18, 67, 125
anti-establishment parties 42,
  43–4, 142
anti-Europeanism 4
anti-imperialism 110
'anywheres' 59
Arendt, Hannah 6
Attlee, Clement 136
Attlee governments 134
Aufstehen 121
austerity 36, 86
authoritarian law and order 47

authoritarians 6
authority 67
automobile designs 21

Bank of England 37
Batson, Daniel 18
benefits, welfare 16, 39, 113,
  116, 118
Berger, Peter L. 159, 160
Bernstein, Eduard 131
biological evolution 88–9
Blair, Tony 121
blame 14, 54–5, 71, 137, 138
blue-collar workers 55, 60
borders, tightening 74, 75
bourgeois self-interest 85
Bowling Alone (Putnam) 60–1
Brexit 4, 55, 64, 66, 69,
  75, 97–8
  and conservatives 43–6
  and low-income citizens
    14, 62–3
  and mobility 161
  voting by social grade 56, 83

Index

Brexit Party 57, 70, 123
Brown, Gordon 121
Burgoon, Brian 158
Burke, Edmund 41
businesses 91, 124, 134–5

Cadwalladr, Carole 54
Cameron government 37
capital 36, 40, 63, 66, 69,
    141, 144
  cultural 113
  and national populism 69
  personal 60
  political 149
capitalism 16, 21–2, 41, 85,
    110, 111, 131
  and feminism 91, 160
  and social democrats
    132, 135
care 67
Central and Eastern Europe 93
change, resistance to 45
child benefit,
    means-testing 37
childcare 92
child poverty 113
Christian Democratic
    Union 33
Christianity 21, 22
civic nationalism 136
civic organizations 65
Civil Service 37
civil society 60–1
class 92
  see also middle classes;
    working classes
climate change 7, 149
collective action 16
collective identity 14
colonialism 110
common good 37–8, 40, 75,
    118, 139

communism 138
communist states 111
compromise 17, 133
conflict 71–2, 74, 110,
    138, 158
conservatism 9, 13–14, 21,
    33–48, 134, 135
  and the environment 149
  and relative deprivation 158
conservative activists 36–7
Conservative governments
    71, 116
Conservative Party 33, 35, 55,
    57–8, 115, 122, 123–4
conservatives 21, 33, 99
cooperation 7, 38
Corbynism 124
Corbyn, Jeremy 15, 108, 113,
    121, 122–3
core voters 118
Cortés, Donoso 45
COVID-19 33, 37, 39, 144
critical junctures 20–1, 144
Crosland, Anthony 134
cross-national research
    designs 159
Crucible, The (Miller) 1
cultural activities 59–60
cultural capital 113
cultural politics 91
cultural views 57

death, fear of 46
death penalty 96, 161
deindustrialization 60
deliberation 6
democracy 15, 61, 97, 99,
    100, 145–6
democratic collective
    action 16
democratic deficits 98
deprivation 65, 67
deregulation 16, 33, 40, 149

destination countries 93
development issues 148–9
discourses 159–60, 165
discrimination 90–1, 100
discursive institutionalism
    22, 119
disorder 41, 44, 47, 74, 134

Eastern Europe 93
Eatwell, Roger 64
Ebbw Vale 55, 59–60,
    63–4, 141
echo chambers 94
economic equality 162
economic externalization 138
economic inequality 89, 90
economic justice 15, 115, 119
economic libertarianism 34,
    36, 41, 45, 47, 83
economic needs 160
economic policies 43, 47
economic security 17
economic views 57
education 59, 69, 83–4, 85
    low 57, 58, 66, 68, 70
Education Department 92
elections 44, 115, 116, 121,
    133, 162
    French presidential *84*
    Spain 108
electric currents 21
elites 16, 19, 91, 111, 120,
    135, 140
emigration 59, 93
    see also immigration
employment 59, 61–2
environmental issues 149
equality 15, 84, 91, 162
equality of opportunity 89
ethics 84, 87–8, 94
ethnic minorities 23, 68,
    90, 141

EU 4, 73, 98, 99–100, 138–9
    Charter of Fundamental
        Rights 98
    funding 55
    membership 46
European Social Survey 158
Euroscepticism 69
evolution 88–9
exit options 59, 65
external conflict 72
external disorder 14
external instability 48
externalization 13–14, 38–9,
    47, 48, 70–1, 97, 99
    and social democrats
        135, 138
external order 43, 138
external stability 138

factory acts 89
fairness 67, 118, 119, 134
false consciousness 66
family life 91–2
Farage, Nigel 14
feminism 91, 92, 160
feminists 108
First Past the Post (FPTP)
    system 108, 123
foreign policy 109
Foucault, Michel 159, 160
FPTP *see* First Past the Post
    (FPTP) system
framing theory 19
France 72, 82, 122, 123, 138
    2017 presidential
        election *84*
France Insoumise, La 108, 123
Fraser, Nancy 91, 160
freedom 87–8
freedom of movement
    92–3, 138–9
free markets 13, 41, 57

Friedman, Milton 32, 36
functionalism 19, 20

Garzón, Alberto 107
Geering, Dominik 113, 162–3
gender equality 91
Germany 164, 165
Gingrich, Jane 117, 163
global cooperation 7
globalization 16, 40, 41, 42,
    47, 58, 75, 133
  backlash against 62
  and Brexit 63
  and COVID-19 144
  and liberalism 97
  and mobility 59
  and New Labour 134–5
  slowing 67–8
  and social democrats 139
  and social liberals 90, 92–5
  and working classes 136–7
global stability 97, 98, 100
Goodhart, David 59
Goodwin, Matthew 64
governing tactic 133
Great Transformation
    (Polanyi) 41
Greece 117
growth, marginal 141–2

Haidt, Jonathan 67
Hakim, Catherine 91
Hampstead wing 145
Hartlepool wing 145
Häusermann, Silja 113,
    117, 162–3
Hayek, Friedrich 36
Help for Heroes 67
historical institutionalism 20
home life 91–2
housing 40, 43, 57, 124
housing benefit 115

human reasoning 3

ideas 88–9, 96, 113, 124, 143,
    159–62, 165
  and discursive
    institutionalism 21–2
  and Mannheim 94
identity 14, 58, 60, 67,
    110, 150
identity politics 161
ideology 18, 100
Ideology and Utopia see
    Mannheim, Karl,
    Ideology and Utopia
IFS *see* Institute for Fiscal
    Studies
immigrants 59, 71
immigration 63–4, 84, 92–3,
    96, 115, 137, 161
  and lower classes 140–1
  and social democrats
    16, 132
  and wages 61–2
imperialism 109, 112
income 39, 42, 83, 84, 116,
    118, 142
  low 14, 62, 68, 70, 115,
    121, 122
  and Conservative Party
    57–8, 123
  and women 92
independence 45
industrial workers 132
inequality 45, 85–6, 89, 90,
    115, 118, 142
  and conservatism 39–40,
    47, 134
  regional 141
  and social democrats 132
  and violent conflict 158
  wealth 132

Index

Inglehart, Ronald 66
instability 41, 48, 71
Institute for Fiscal Studies
    (IFS) 116–17, 118, 163
institutionalism 22, 119
institutional rupture 110
institutional theory 19,
    20–2, 46
institutions, preservation 41
instrumental rationality 69
internal conflict 72
internal disorder 14
internal instability 48
internal order 43, 138
international conflict 138
international
    externalization 138
internationalism 100, 136
international justice 112
international organizations
    98, 138–9
interventionism 57, 145
intimidation 125
isolationism 74, 110, 138
Israel 4, 109

Johnson, Boris 34, 44, 123–4
Johnson government 57–8
justice 15, 112, 115, 119

Kaczyński, Jarosław 68
Kazzia 32
Kołakowski, Leszek 131
Kriesi et al 59, 160

Labour governments 134, 136
Labour manifesto 117
labour market policy 43
Labour moderates 16
Labour Party 115, 116, 121,
    122, 132, 133, 145
    Corbyn 108, 113

and socio-cultural
    professionals 123
    Starmer 109
Law and Justice (PiS)
    government 57, 123
Leave campaign 46, 83
Leave voters 23, 55, 63
left, the, radical 42, 108, 136,
    137–8, 158
left-wing movements 4
left-wing parties 108, 162
leisure time 85
Le Pen, Jean-Marie 73
LGBT+ activists 108
LGBT+ rights 95, 96, 115
liberal democracy 6, 145–6
liberal-democratic
    institutions 41
liberal-democratic public
    sphere 6
Liberal Democrats 16, 86, 117
liberalism *11*, 14–15, 82–100,
    137, 160–2
liberal multilateralism 138
Lipset, Seymour Martin 66
living standards 42, 43, 142
local conditions 14, 140–1
localities 34, 59–60, 64, 75,
    93, 140, 161
lower classes 57, 65–6, 69, 70,
    92, 108, 115
    attachment to place
        136, 140
    and capitalism 132
    and Remain vote 23
    and social democrats 137
    see also working classes
lower-middle classes 43,
    56, 142
low-income and education
    voters 14, 44, 57–8,
    62, 68, 70

Index

low-income communities
61–3
low status 67
loyalty 67
Luckmann, Thomas 159, 160

Macmillan, Harold 41
Macron, Emmanuel 82
Manifesto Project 163–4
manifestos 163–4
Mannheim, Karl 94, 100
Ideology and Utopia 87
marginal growth 141–2
market liberalization 13,
41–2, 57
Marxists 21, 66, 83, 109, 110,
111, 135
Marx, Karl 85, 107, 120
mass migration 61–2
Matthews, Kent 98
Mélenchon, Jean-Luc 107,
119, 120, 122
middle classes 42, 43, 56, 93,
113, 116–17, 119, 142
and abolition of tuition
fees 16
young 15, 39, 107, 109
middle-income groups 43
migration 61–2, 121
see also immigration
minorities 71–2, 82, 88, 115,
123, 137, 138
mobility 58, 59, 65, 92, 93,
140, 160
morality 85
mothers, working 92
multilateralism, liberal 97
Muslims 71, 72

national democracy 15, 97,
99, 100
national identity 58

nationalism 69, 136, 138, 161
national populism *10*, 14, 39,
54–75, 97, 132, 160–1
and climate denial 149
increases internal and
external tension 48, 137
and international
conflict 138
and redistribution 123
and relative
deprivation 157–8
and social democracy 145
national-populist movements
4, 43–4
national-populist parties 98–9
NATO 73, 138
New Labour 118, 121,
135, 137
new left *11*, 15–16, 21,
107–25, 138, 162–3
and social democracy 132,
135, 145
new-left parties 98–9
no deal Brexit 63, 69
non-material terms 2–3, 34,
57, 58, 62, 109
Norris, Pippa 66

obesity 40
objective reality 159
openness 90
opportunity, equality 89
order 40–1, 46, 138
othering 74, 138

party supporters 114,
115–16, 164
PASOK (Greece) *133*
path dependency 21, 144
patriotism 67, 136
pay cap, public sector 117